Napa Valley
CHRONICLES

Napa Valley
CHRONICLES

LAUREN COODLEY

THE History PRESS

Published by The History Press
Charleston, SC 29403
www.historypress.net

Back cover image: Buhman Oaks, by Heli Sairanen.

First published 2013

Manufactured in the United States

ISBN 978.1.60949.926.6

Library of Congress CIP data applied for.

Contents

Acknowledgements 7
"Brown Street," by Paula Amen Judah 9

Prelude to Part I 11
1. Nineteenth Century
Retracing Juliana's Path 15
"The Sky's Blue Looking-Glass":
Rediscovering Robert Louis Stevenson 19
Stories of Suffrage 22
2. Early Twentieth Century
Turn-of-the-Century Downtown 27
A Japanese Journey 32
Time Passing in Napa 37
3. The 1920s
Voices from Early Browns Valley 43
Napa's Roaring Twenties 47
A Tannery in a Town, I and II 51
4. The 1930s
Two Love Stories from Dunn Lee Manor 57
Discovering Rita Bordwell, I and II 62
Every Memory a Door 68
5. The 1940s
Listening for Trains 73

Following the Trail 77
The Construction of History, I and II 81

PRELUDE TO PART II 89
6. The 1950s
"History Isn't Always Taught Properly":
The Legacy of Ivy Loeber 93
Napa's Unknown Brenda Starr 98
What West Park Was 102
7. The 1960s
Searching for Peggy Connolly 107
Remembering Napa's Service Stations 110
Fancy Faire and Community Projects 113
8. The 1970s
Feminism Finds Napa 117
Mrs. Brewster's Double Life 121
Treasures of Terrace Drive 126
9. The Way We Live Today
A Fine State of Perfection: Dr. Phong Vu's
Napa Childhood 133
Maria's Story 137
A Collins Family Christmas 142

Epilogue 147
Notes 151
About the Author 160

Acknowledgements

Many people in my community have assisted on these essays, contributing research, memories, ideas and suggestions. Cathy Mathews, whose father raised prunes on Monticello Road and worked at Basalt, has served as informant, reporter and commentator, and you will find her pithy insights throughout the book. Stephanie Grohs, who grew up in the West Park neighborhood, has helped me to imagine Napa as it was before I had ever been here. Together, we developed a unique class on the history of this region that was once taught at the community college. Stephanie's research on the African American and Japanese presence in the Napa Valley has been immensely helpful to both me and other scholars, and she also appears in some of the stories in this volume.

Those many people who donated reminiscences or photographs are acknowledged in the notes at the end of the book. Each of the articles in this book has its own bibliography for you to peruse. I would like to particularly thank Peter Manasse, Nilan Kincaid, Napa Firefighters Museum, the Napa County Historical Society, the Merry Mariners, Carolyn Knieff Salazar, Liz Reyna, Maria Esparza, Rachel Friedman, Sheryl Collins, Betty Hopperstad, Barbara Mannering, Deb Jachens, Jana Martinez, Marilyn Warnock, Lorie Saxon and Roger Andrews. Friends who have supported my work deserve to be acknowledged: Anita Catlin, Tammy and Jay Rogers, Kenny Drost and Pat Dwyer, Gray Brechin, Pat Wagner and, finally, the two historians of home who have most influenced me: Joseph Amato and Carol Kammen.

My most significant collaborator has been Paula Amen Judah, who grew up on Hoffman Avenue. She is the co-author of the essay about Community Projects, Inc., and has edited many of the essays, which has improved them immensely. Her exquisite poem begins this collection. I can't begin to thank her enough for her clarity, charity and impeccable taste.

I want to thank Connie Anderson and the staff of *Napa Valley Marketplace* for publishing my work over these many years. Thanks also to Aubrie Koenig, my editor at The History Press, for her faith in my project. Appreciations to those who assisted me in creating this manuscript: Lauren Ellsworth, Beth Schultz, Melissa May and, most of all, Adrianna Schwartz.

I work in the past, but I live in the present, thanks to my beautiful grandsons who share this time and place with me and their parents. I dedicate this book to the Vega family, who will live in a future in which I hope this book may serve as a guide and a remembrance.

Brown Street

by Paula Amen Judah

I want to walk
with my mother on
Brown Street again,
catch the breath of
clothy steam from
Money's Cleaners,
hear the bell jingling
against the thick glass door as
patrons come and go,
see Mr. Money
counting out change
into the cupped hands of children
sent in to pick up
their father's slacks.

I want to shade my
eyes against the
dark blue glint of
the tiles that line the
front of the Napa P.D.
where I posed
limp-shouldered
and alone in
my Easter bonnet,
chin and mouth
turned down, beneath
the shadow of my
sister's stiff refusal
to enter the picture.

Brown Street

I want to walk
with my mother on
Brown Street again,
visit the wide lobby
of the Plaza Hotel,
its overstuffed chairs with
their rough upholstery
sitting just inside the door,
the smell of bourbon
trailing over from
Novelli's bar where
through a red straw
I tasted my first
Shirley Temple,
waiting in the muted light with dad
and the rest of the cops
for the bus to the 49er game.

I want to run
with my mother
across Brown Street
in the early morning,
skip up the stairs of
the old Court House
past suited lawyers
and punctual clerks
and men in overalls,
want to hear again
the echo of footsteps
on marble floors, the
sound of the bailiff's
steady *All rise*,
the strike of the
gavel's authority
on dark wood.
I want to inhale the
air of that reliable
building and stop
to read the gold print
on the windowed doors:
  Assessor
  Superior Court

I want to walk with my mother
on Brown Street again.

Prelude to Part I

Step back with me into 1920s Napa, a small town of many cultures, where Chinese immigrants moved out of quicksilver mines and into orchards and tanneries. They built the stone walls and bridges that you can still see throughout the valley. Napa's "Chinatown" consisted of rows of fragile wood-frame dwellings located near what later became the parking lot of the Cinedome movie theater. Walking past these buildings in 1920, you could smell the incense from the Joss House and hear the hiss of the hot irons inside the Sam Yee Laundry on Main Street.

Napa's "Spanishtown" was located among the streets named for some of the Californios who were given land grants by the Mexican government: Yount, Vallejo, Yajome and Juarez. Descendants of the Californios remained in these neighborhoods after the war with Mexico. Some married the indigenous people of the valley, the Meyank-mah. The men often worked as laborers, while many of their wives operated boardinghouses just north of downtown.

East Napa was home to a thriving "Little Italy." Italians built houses with two kitchens, one in the basement and another on the upper floor where the women could cook when the river flooded. Dave Cavagnaro was the unofficial mayor of Little Italy. Cavagnaro organized the famous Fourth of July parades and spent three months every year traveling with the circus. Across from Cavagnaro's hotel, Theresa Tamburelli and her husband ran the Depot restaurant. The Depot had been the cultural and political center of the town's thriving immigrant community of Italian laborers, men who lived at the Brooklyn and Roma Hotels and played bocce ball at the edge of the river. In 1930, while cooking for a visiting team of San Francisco baseball players, Mrs. Tamburelli ran out of pasta dough. Remembering her mother's resourceful cooking, she boiled up tiny dumplings of ravioli filling and called it "malfatti."

Chinese children living in Napa, early twentieth century. *Courtesy of Napa County Historical Society.*

Back then, you could step out of the Depot and board the electric train, which you could ride all the way up to Calistoga or travel south to the Vallejo wharf. "Young man, come west to Napa to start a factory!" read one brochure from this era. The essays in this book chronicle how, by the 1930s, Julian Weidler had brought Rough Rider north from San Francisco and built a clothing factory across the street from the Depot. In that era, Napa High taught its girls how to operate the power sewing machines so that they could get jobs after graduation. At the same time, Sawyer Tannery, across the river, was inventing new kinds of leather for baseball and softball mitts. Shoes were made, shirts were sewed and basalt was quarried in these years. If you sat down to eat at the Depot, you could look across the river and see the ships steaming up and down from the factory, headed for the Panama Canal, or hear the gleaming locomotives whisking Napans down to the ferries or up to the spas.

In the 1920s, my grandparents were courting in Los Angeles. That city, forty years earlier, had shared the population and the gentle rhythms of Napa. I have been watching the changes in Napa since I arrived to be a teacher in 1975. I have been writing about them for the past dozen years.

Olamae Wade (second from right) with her mother, Mary Etta Wade, and siblings. *Courtesy of Olamae Combellack.*

My first book, *Napa: The Transformation of an American Town*, was celebrated at the Depot in 2004. That restaurant is now closed, yet the area that surrounds it has been given new life as a crossroads for visitors from all over the world.

For this volume, I have organized my stories chronologically. My topics range from unknown people like Juliana Salazar to famous ones, like Robert Louis Stevenson. While some of my articles uncover the stories of individuals like Peggy Connolly and Henry Luhmann, others offer glimpses of life on Main Street, of rural Browns Valley, of the railroad, of the Sawyer Tannery. Still other articles were prompted by letters that I received, places I've visited and wondered about or chance remarks heard in the course of my day. Many lives have passed through this town on the river of time. I hope you enjoy meeting some of them.

Chapter 1
NINETEENTH CENTURY

RETRACING JULIANA'S PATH

Historians' decisions about where to begin and end impart shape, meaning, and significance to their narratives; they enable readers to make connections to other stories, or invite readers to reconsider old assumptions.
—Fred Anderson, "America: Into the Heart of Darkness,"
New York Review of Books

Written history of the first female settlers in the Napa Valley is rare, and even rarer is history of Mexican women. What we know about the woman who began her life as Maria Juliana Salazar is far less than what we don't know. She was born in Taos, New Mexico, in 1810. Thirty-four years before she was born, the Declaration of Independence was written on America's eastern coast while Franciscan friars Dominguez and Escalante explored routes from New Mexico to California. Just three years before her birth, Zebulon Pike led the first Anglo-American expedition into New Mexico.

We know nothing of her childhood and adolescence. She is listed in public records through marriages and her children's births. By the age of twenty-four, she was twice widowed with two young children and was known as Juliana Rodriguez. That year, 1834, she met Julian Pope, who would become her third husband. Pope had left Kentucky at the age of seventeen to hunt and trade in the Mexican territory that would become New Mexico. He joined George Yount's trapping expedition in 1827. In 1830, the Mexican government restricted trapping by

Yount migrated to California in 1833. After he served in the Mexican army, General Vallejo gave him almost twelve thousand acres as a land grant. *Courtesy of Napa County Historical Society.*

non-Mexican citizens. Thus, William Pope, as he had been christened, set about becoming a Mexican citizen. He joined the Catholic Church, changed his name from William to Julian and began investing in the trade of woolen blankets for the California mules that passed between New Mexico and California.

Julian Pope and Juliana Rodriguez were married at San Geronimo de Taos in New Mexico. In 1835, they joined a trading caravan and moved to Los Angeles, where Juliana gave birth to two daughters, Luciana and Isabella. In 1838, Julian Pope received a parcel of land east of the city in the area later known as Boyle Heights, where he built a house and planted seeds. The next year, he erected a gristmill on a bank of the Los Angeles River below the road leading to the San Gabriel mission.

Hearing of the vast land grants awarded by General Mariano Vallejo in northern California, Julian Pope joined an expedition to the Napa Valley in 1841. Along with friends, who included Cyrus Alexander, William Knight and William Gordon, he crossed the Carquinez Straits in a rowboat. They hired indigenous men to pilot them up the Napa River. After making base camp at Yount's home, in the area that would eventually be called Yountville, the four split up, each claiming a valley as his own. Pope petitioned General Vallejo and Manuel Casarin, the acting governor of California, for a parcel on the east side of Howell Mountain. The parcel, almost nine thousand acres, cost him twenty-five cents, and Pope named his grant "Rancho Locoallomi." Juliana and the four children moved from Los Angeles and stayed at Yount's ranch while Julian built their first home on his new property. The Mexican government paid for the family's expenses because it wanted the help of settlers like the Popes to subdue the indigenous tribes. Scholar Linda Heidenreich writes, "In Napa, Indigenous histories, Californiana/o histories, Euro-American histories, and Chinese and

George Yount built this blockhouse and adobe dwelling in 1837. That year, he also built the first flour mill in the valley. *Courtesy of Napa County Historical Society.*

Mexican immigrant histories co-exist. At times they overlap and/or conflict with each other. But they always co-exist."

In 1842, at Yount's ranch, Juliana gave birth to her fifth child, Delavina. In 1843, the family moved wagons and livestock from Yount's ranch to their new adobe house, using ropes to ease the wagons down the steep trail. Tragically, that same year, Julian was rushing to complete a wooden house before winter and accidentally cut his leg when his axe slipped. According to one story, he was carried all the way to Sonoma for medical attention. Twelve days later, at the age of thirty-eight, he died.

Juliana was now thirty-three years old. The following spring, in 1844, she married her nearest neighbor, Elias Barnett, a Missouri pioneer who brought the first fruit tree seedlings from Missouri to Calistoga. Juliana Pope Barnett took legal possession of Pope's land in 1845. In order to do so, she met the Mexican civil authorities with her husband, Elias, along with Florencio Salazar, Joseph Chiles and her surveyor, Juan Solis. Solis and George Yount, acting as surveyor for the mayor of Sonoma, measured the boundaries of the property. At each of the four corners of the property, the story goes, Juliana pulled up stones and grass and threw them to the four winds, a ritual to declare her possession of the land.

In this period when California was a Mexican state, women like Juliana ran the ranchos while the men were away. They were trained in horseback riding and in the use of small arms to protect themselves. Like all married

Jesse Barnett's father, Elias, married Juliana Salazar Pope. The Barnetts raised cattle, horses, sheep and hogs. *Courtesy of Napa County Historical Society.*

women in the nineteenth century, Juliana was pregnant most of her adult life. Juliana had six more children with Barnett, including two sets of twins in 1845 and 1854. By then she had borne eleven children. Juliana and her husband also adopted three Indian children.

In 1850, California was admitted as the fiftieth state in the Union. In 1854, Juliana Pope Barnett sold half of the land and "100 head of cattle, 15 mares and 9 colts" to her eldest son, Jose, for $8,000. She sold the other half of the land to her other five children for $5,000. At that point, she left Pope Valley, so perhaps she sold her land to finance her relocation. Further research might illuminate why Juliana was able to leave her husband in an era in which women rarely did so.

We don't know where Juliana lived for the next six years. Her granddaughters reported that she painted nudes, which hung in the bars of San Francisco during the gold rush. By 1860, the U.S. Census records Juliana as a "female farmer" living in San Bernardino with her daughter Isabella Pope; her son Jose lived next door. In 1880, she is listed in the census as living with daughter Luciana in Las Cruces, New Mexico. According to the Society of California Pioneers, her husband, Elias Barnett, died on February 8, 1880 in Pope Valley, where he had remained for all the years after Juliana moved away. Juliana Salazar Rodriguez Pope Barnett died in 1900, at ninety years of age. None of her paintings is known to have survived, nor did she leave any written accounts of her life. Therefore, we can only mourn the absence of a more complete record and be grateful for those who have attempted to retrace her path.

"THE SKY'S BLUE LOOKING-GLASS": REDISCOVERING ROBERT LOUIS STEVENSON

Up into the cherry tree
Who should climb but little me?
I held the trunk with both my hands
And looked abroad in foreign lands.
I saw the next door garden lie,
Adorned with flowers, before my eye,
And many pleasant places more
That I had never seen before.
—R.L.S.

I have loved the poems of Robert Louis Stevenson since I grew up hearing them sung on an LP record. Decades later, I recited them with my own children. Thus, the brief intersection of Stevenson's life with that of the Napa Valley is of great interest to me.

Robert Louis Stevenson was born in 1850. In the exquisite museum illustrating his life in St. Helena, the visitor learns that he had a Victorian childhood—boys played with tea sets and dolls, preserved at the museum, along with his lead soldiers. His nursemaid didn't cut his hair until he was four and a half years old. That first haircut is also preserved at the museum, along with a curl of hair from his nursemaid, Alison Cunningham, to whom he would later dedicate *A Child's Garden of Verses.*

Stevenson's father, Thomas, was a civil engineer, specializing in the development of new technology for Scotland's many lighthouses. Stevenson dedicated his *Familiar Studies of Men and Books*, "To Thomas Stevenson, civil engineer, by whose devices the great sea lights in every quarter of the world now shine more brightly." His mother, Margaret Balfour Stevenson, kept a journal of her child's doings, his games and toys. She embraced a view of childhood that was controversial in its day. Mrs. Stevenson admired Froebel, a German educator who thought that children should not be treated as little beings born in sin but that childhood should be a time of gentle growth toward happy and sociable maturity.

In 1876, as a young man, Stevenson traveled to Paris and met a married American woman and mother of three, Fanny Van de Grift Osbourne. Although they were ten years apart in age, the two became friends and, eventually, romantically involved. In August 1879, Fanny returned to Oakland to obtain a divorce. Stevenson sailed from Scotland for America in hopes of persuading her to marry him.

Though he considered the voyage a grand adventure, Stevenson's friends were worried that it would affect his fragile health. He traveled by steamship to New York and on to California by train, becoming more ill with each mile. He was near death when he arrived in Monterey. By December 1879, Stevenson had recovered his health enough to continue to San Francisco.

In the nineteenth century, produce wagons were hauled by mule teams with provisions for travelers. *Courtesy of Napa County Historical Society.*

Fanny, now divorced and recovered from her own illness, found him still very weak and nursed him to recovery. When they married, his family cut off his trust fund.

In 1880, the couple enjoyed what writer M.F.K. Fisher describes as a few "poignant and enchanted months in the Northern California valley named Napa by its vanished Indians." In his memoir of their visit, Stevenson offers a rare picture of the Napa Valley in the late nineteenth century:

> *Bucks, bears and rattlesnakes and former mining operations, are the staple of men's talk. Agriculture has only begun to mount above the valley and though in a few years from now the whole district may be smiling with farms, passing trains shaking the mountain to the heart, many windowed hotels lighting up the night like factories, and a prosperous city occupying the site of sleepy Calistoga; yet in the meantime, around the foot of that mountain the silence of nature reigns in a great measure unbroken.*

With determination to overcome the daunting challenge of renovating an abandoned bunkhouse high up on Mount St. Helena, the Stevensons were delivered by stagecoach to their new home on the mountain. Fanny mended the bunker while he wrote. A few months later, his parents relented, so the

This farming scene from a postcard shows what R.L. Stevenson would have observed as he traveled up the valley toward Calistoga. *Courtesy of Mr. M.*

Stevensons returned to the British Isles. Robert Louis Stevenson wrote first *Treasure Island* (1883) and then *A Child's Garden of Verses* (1885). About this book, Canadian scholar Elizabeth Waterston writes:

> *The poems recall exactly the earliest responses to language: the delight in reiteration, the pleasure at new words. "The Swing," for instance, catches the child's fondness for repetition: "Up in the air and over the wall, up in the air and down"—that last phrase adding the joy of antithesis and surprise.*

Within this beautiful collection, we can find suggestions of the influence of the Napa Valley on Robert Lewis Stevenson. Cherry trees grew plentifully in this "foreign land," and he writes:

I saw the dimpling river pass
And be the sky's blue looking-glass;
The dusty roads go up and down
With people tramping in to town.
If I could find a higher tree
Farther and farther I should see
To where the grown-up river slips
Into the sea among the ships.

STORIES OF SUFFRAGE

Failure is impossible.
—Susan B. Anthony, Final Speech

How did the right to vote get extended to all citizens of Napa? When did African American men begin voting? What about equal suffrage for women?

Sharon McGriff-Payne's survey of property records and census figures reveals that two to three hundred African Americans lived in Napa County between the 1860s and the 1890s. The African Methodist Episcopal Church, founded in 1867, was one of the first in California. The building stood on Washington Street between First and Clay. In addition to providing a place of worship, the church offered educational opportunities for children of its members. *Uncle Tom's Cabin*, a play based on abolitionist Harriet Beecher Stowe's antislavery novel, was staged in

The Fifteenth Amendment. Celebrated May 19th, 1870. From an original design by James C. Beard. Published by Thomas Kelly, New York, circa 1870. *Courtesy of the Library of Congress, Prints and Photographs Division, Washington, D.C.*

Vallejo also in 1867. Napans might have traveled the eleven miles by horse and buggy to attend the performance.

On February 3, 1870, the Fifteenth Amendment to the Constitution was ratified, prohibiting states from denying citizens the right to vote based on "race, color, or previous condition of servitude." Black churches in the Napa and Vallejo areas, along with those around the country, celebrated. The amendment expanded voting rights, but only to newly emancipated men. On April 11, 1870, Napa's black residents gathered to celebrate with a speech given by Reverend William R. Hillary, dancing and hundred-gun salute, all at Napa Hall.

Frederick Sparrow was undoubtedly one of those attending the celebration. Sparrow owned a barbershop at 52 Main Street in Napa. Black barbers served a primarily white clientele. McGriff-Payne notes that "such business ownership not only allowed African-American men a level of independence, it gave them a prestige within the community that was nearly unprecedented." McGriff-Payne describes how "in April 1870, Frederick A. Sparrow strode the short distance from his home to the Napa County Courthouse where he registered to vote for the first time."

The ongoing struggle to gain voting rights for American women would surely affect the future of Frederick Sparrow's female descendants. In 1896, California men cast votes on whether to extend suffrage to women. The campaign for women's suffrage sent Susan B. Anthony to Napa that year. Anthony was born a Quaker, the first denomination to denounce slavery and to actively work against it in the abolitionist movement. Women were not allowed to speak in public; for the female abolitionists, their struggle against slavery became a struggle for women's rights as well.

Anthony was seventy-six years old when she came to Napa. She probably traveled in a steamer boat from San Francisco right up the Napa River and may have stepped off the dock where the Third Street Bridge is now. The *Napa Register* reported that she spoke to enthusiastic crowds throughout our county. The next day, the Reverend Anna Howard Shaw spoke. Along with Anthony, Shaw had been working to get the vote for women for more than forty years. She became a teacher at the age of fifteen. There was a movement to license women to preach in the Methodist church; the presiding elder in her district invited her to preach a sermon when she was twenty-three years old. Later, she became a full-time organizer for women's suffrage. She was sent to Napa as president of the National American Women's Suffrage Association.

Reporters described the local suffrage conference held at the Opera House a month later. A Mrs. Mills stated, "The anti's are in the minority in California; California has such excellent men; and the press in California favors equal suffrage." Mrs. B.F. Taylor added, "We cannot claim that our Constitution is of the people, by the people and for the people when one half of them are disenfranchised." But the suffrage ballot measure of 1896 failed by a large margin. Considering the state's powerful saloon and liquor interests, "and the myth that voting women would shut down the liquor lobby, it was no wonder that the 1896 Suffrage Amendment failed," historian Mae Silver notes. Suffrage activists had neither the propaganda skill nor the resources to meet the demands of campaigning to such a large and diverse citizenry.

Susan B. Anthony came back to San Francisco in 1902 as the lead speaker of the annual convention of the California Woman's Suffrage Association. She was then eighty years old. She died in 1906 without ever being able to vote. At her funeral services, the Reverend Anna Howard

Suffrage map. *Courtesy of Mae Silver.*

Shaw spoke: "To her, the cause was everything; she knew no existence apart from it…It was the first and last thought of each day; it was the last word upon her faltering lips."

Political science should be anything but a dull subject. The struggles of Americans to be able to vote as full citizens captivate the imagination. For us in Napa, we can now imagine Frederick Sparrow striding into the courtroom to cast his first ballot in 1870 or Susan B. Anthony getting off the steamer at the Third Street dock in 1896.

Chapter 2
EARLY TWENTIETH CENTURY

TURN-OF-THE-CENTURY DOWNTOWN

History is two things: it is the past, and it is what happens in the minds of historians who bring to the documents their own interests and concerns, as well as the interests, concerns, and historical understandings of their eras.
—Carol Kammen, On Doing Local History

Charles Otterson came to Napa to run the electric car barns. He became a building inspector in 1906 and was also chosen as Napa's first fire chief, a job he would proudly hold until 1943. Every year, Napa's volunteer firefighters held a Fourth of July parade. Between 1904 and 1907, Carl Browne produced the *Napa Cartoon Cactus* and served as its publisher, editor, cartoonist and writer. He was a fervent supporter of the progressive reforms of President Theodore Roosevelt and specifically praised Upton Sinclair's exposé of the meatpacking industry. Browne was given a place of honor in the 1907 Fourth of July parade.

Elmer Bickford bought one of the town's first automobiles, an Oldsmobile, in 1904. He and his wife, Ada, had two children: Ruth in 1907 and Robert in 1904. Bickford co-founded the Boy Scouts of Napa. When he took the Scouts bird-watching at Tulocay Cemetery, Big and Little Trancas, McKenzie's Nursery on Waterworks Road and the bridge west of Union Station, they recorded seventy-six species of birds. Some of these birds that are no longer here include the tule wren, the western sandpiper, the spoonbill duck and the sparrow hawk.

Mildred Pearch (left) and Ruth Bickford (right) in 1921 on Madison Street. Ruth was born in the house behind the car. *Courtesy of Robert Northrup.*

The California Glove Company, which had opened in 1876, eventually employed five hundred people in two factories making work gloves, driving gloves and ladies' fine dress gloves. Cameron Shirt Company opened in 1901 and produced one hundred dozen work shirts in a day. With a population of five thousand people, Napa had only a few telephones and one operator, Mary Stoddard. When Stoddard left in 1900 to take a position with Sawyer Tannery, the *Napa Daily Journal* urged citizens to be patient "until the new operator becomes accustomed to the names of the subscribers."

On the outskirts of town, dairy farming was widespread. One major farm was the Ambrosia Dairy, developed by William Watt, who, like Chief Otterson, came to Napa in 1906. Watt purchased part of Salvador Vallejo's land grant. He decided to manufacture ice cream and produced thousands of gallons every summer. Watt's Creamery wagons traveled daily through Napa, Sonoma and Solano Counties. One of his main sources of milk was from Manuel Almada, whose dairy farm in Soscol was on the land that had once belonged to Mariano Vallejo. Henry Wigger told interviewer Laura Thomas that within the town itself,

> *Everybody had their own milk cows, chickens, and vegetable gardens. Frank Noyes had a cow up there where the Bank of America on First Street is*

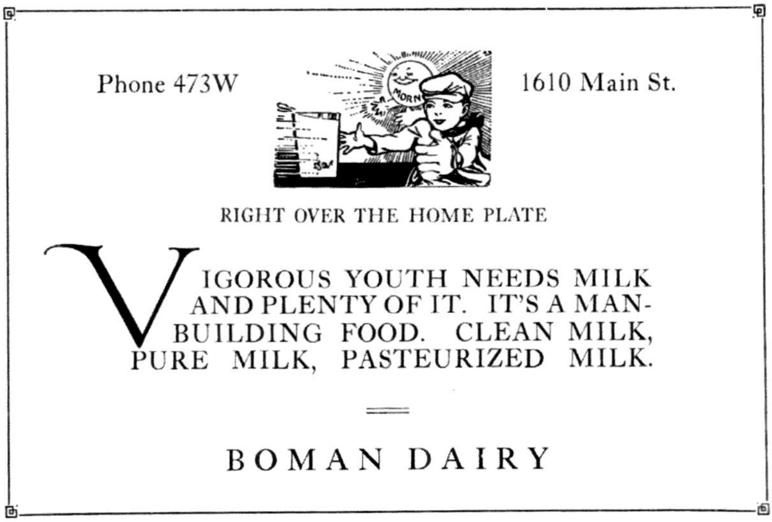

Have you a nice creepy book?
Yes. Are you a bookworm?

The *San Francisco Chronicle* reported in 1923 that there were nineteen thousand dairy cows in Napa County, most of them in the southwestern part of the county. *From the 1924* Napanee, *courtesy of Robert Northrup.*

> *now... There was the Napa City Bakery owned by the Stoll family. Keig's Shoe Store went all the way from Main to Brown Street; you could get anything you wanted in fine footwear. Across the creek was China Town. We used to go there and get a dried abalone for a nickel.*

Napa High School opened in 1897. In 1910, the front cover of the *Napanee* yearbook featured an ad for Herman Schwartz's Hardware Store, advertising 150 different pairs of pocketknives and "beautiful lamps for gas, oil or electric." The inside back cover carried an ad for the Napa Coffee Club, advertising "free reading and rest room, a complete dinner for $.25 on Second Street opposite the Court House." At her 1911 graduation, senior class president Dorothy Coombs wrote:

> *Many things we were to learn in that queer brown building with its falling plaster, cracking floors and narrow stairs. With this scenery we played our part for two eventful years. At first the boys and girls were separated, for better or worse, probably the latter, for the order did not seem to improve.*

This yearbook advertises Joseph Levinson as the "Leading Druggist." Joe Levinson's parents, Freedman Levinson and his wife, Dora, had traveled on foot across the Panama Isthmus into Central America and then up through Mexico during the gold rush. Freedman Levinson opened a small general store on Main Street, where business was usually conducted in gold dust. The family lived within walking distance of the store.

Son Joe opened Levinson's Pharmacy on the corner of Main and First, offering the only X-ray machine in town. Joe's sister Sarah was said to have made so many doses of chicken soup that she actually wore a dent in the table where she rolled her homemade noodles. Joe's brother Charlie opened Levinson's clothing store on Main Street and was an active member of the Unity Volunteer Hose Company. When he became part of the paid fire department in 1906, he offered Jewish families a room to worship on the firehouse's top floor. Joe's sister Clara married an Englishman she met at a Unity Hose Company dance, and they set up a tobacco shop next to Charlie's clothing store.

The yearbook lists the Popular Dining Room on 13–15 Main Street as the "Leading Restaurant of Napa." Unadvertised in the yearbooks was the fact that both sides of Clinton Street were lined with houses of prostitution, possibly as many as twenty. When east Napa flooded in 1909, some of the women stepped out to swim in the floodwaters. When the city granted liquor licenses to these businesses, citizens wrote to complain, not about the business of prostitution, but about the liquor licenses. Reporter Charles Johnson writes:

> *The girls, usually well-dressed, were often seen alone or in pairs walking down Main Street on shopping tours. They rarely if ever used the street to make appointments. They were of course never seen in bars or other low places, which in those days were strictly reserved for men.*

Johnson saw prostitution as "a necessary function of society like barbering or horseshoeing" and noted that community leaders "thought nothing of parking their easily identifiable buggies in front of the Clinton Street houses." Mae Howard was one of the most famous madams in an era when women ran prostitution and police were often tolerant.

Other women continued to work for full rights of citizenship in the hope that the female vote would raise wages and end prostitution. In 1911, suffrage was again on the ballot. This time, the College Equal Suffrage League campaigned in a special car named the Blue Liner. Feminist historian Mae

Adolph Spreckels raised show horses, including the famous Seabiscuit, at his estate just south of downtown Napa (now River Park). *Courtesy of Mr. M.*

Silver writes, "Trimmed like a pet horse, the car sported yellow streamers and was especially appealing to men." We don't have evidence yet on whether the Blue Liner came to Napa, but I think it is likely. The suffragists were supported by the newspaper *The Call*, edited by a son of the sugar millionaire Claus Spreckels, whose brother Adolph had a racehorse farm in south Napa. After the October 10 election, both leading San Francisco papers declared suffrage defeated, but *The Call* reminded readers that the vote had not yet been counted. *The Call* predicted that suffrage would win with 4,000 votes; in the final tally, it won with 3,587 votes. In gratitude for the victory, the Equal Suffrage League wrote:

But from the strength of the hills
Men's voices hailed us;
God bless our farmer-folk,
Scarce a man failed us!

Elmer Bickford's daughter Ruth was one of many women to benefit from suffrage. After graduation, she attended Cal Berkeley by taking the electric train to Vallejo, a ferry across the Carquinez Straits and another electric train from Crockett all the way to campus. She became the president of the Napa Historical Society. In the early 1980s, I invited her to talk to my child's second-grade class about her memories of old Napa, little knowing that later I would find her notes for that talk, carefully preserved on index cards among her yearbooks and diaries.

A JAPANESE JOURNEY

Yes, spring has come
This morning a nameless hill
Is shrouded in mist.
—Basho, 1660

How many Japanese immigrants were living in California at the turn of the nineteenth century? What were the chances that one of them would travel to Napa and that his son would record the story of that trip? Just such a journey was documented when Clarence Iwao Nishizu was interviewed in 1982 about his immigrant father's experience working at a St. Helena vineyard. In 1902, Clarence's father, Nobujiro Nishizu, traveled from the village of Tachibana to San Francisco:

> *He went to work on a farm for a person by the name of Wheeler in Napa County, at a place called Zinfandel Lane, near the town of St. Helena. My uncle was there too. He worked for Mr. Wheeler who became rich by inventing and making cream of tartar.*

By 1900, about two thousand Japanese immigrants already lived in San Francisco, while five hundred or so had found a home in Southern California. Japanese laborers began to be increasingly important to the success of California agriculture. Yet, like the Chinese before them, they were viewed with suspicion. Lin Weber's examination of the *Napa Daily Journal* in 1904 reveals that "the few citizens with the courage to oppose public opinion did so at some peril. The Wheeler family allowed a number of Japanese workers to live on their ranch on Zinfandel Lane. Threats were made, and it was feared that 'strong sentiment in certain corners' would result in violence."

The Wheeler family chose to ignore the pressure, and John Wheeler encouraged Mr. Nishizu to bring other neighbors and relatives to work on the farm. Mr. Nishizu's son Clarence describes two of them:

Two Japanese American men in front of the Napa train station. *Courtesy of the Department of Special Collections and University Archives, California State University–Sacramento.*

Taichiro Ueno and Mr. Koheiji Fujino came to Napa at the age of sixteen. My father told me that Koheiji was more interested in leaning on the shovel and talking to his fellow countrymen than working. One day Mr. Wheeler told my father to send Koheiji over to his house so he could work as a school boy [live-in worker] *and help in domestic duties around the house.*

Mr. Wheeler traveled daily from St. Helena to San Francisco, where he took young Fujino to study at the grammar school there. Most likely, the two traveled on the Southern Pacific Railroad, boarding in St. Helena and disembarking in Vallejo, where they could ride a ferry across the bay.

Once they arrived in San Francisco, they could take a streetcar to their destinations. After he finished school, Fujino would go to the Bohemian Club on Taylor Street, of which Mr. Wheeler was a member. As Clarence Nishizu heard it from his father:

> *While he waited at the Bohemian Club, the ambitious Fujino learned the art of mixing drinks for the customers and became a good bartender, practicing English at the same time. When Mr. Wheeler returned, Fujino would ride back with him to their residence in St. Helena where he helped with the cooking and other household duties.*

Clarence Nishizu always remembers a story about the fabled Fujino:

> *One night young Fujino came and banged on the door of the bunkhouse where everyone had just gone into bed and said, "I got a chicken here, let's eat some chicken gohan." Gohan is rice cooked with shoyu, which is a special dish in Kasuya Gun. Everybody got out of bed, cut the chicken's head off and enjoyed the chicken gohan and had a grand time. Apparently, young Fujino was tired of eating American dishes at the Wheeler residence. He was supposed to go back to the Wheeler house that night, but he pleaded with his friends to let him stay overnight.*

One of the casualties of the San Francisco earthquake in 1906 was John Wheeler's cream of tartar works, destroyed in the fires. Nobujiro Nishizu left St. Helena for Colorado, hoping to go into farming for himself. He ended up working as a sharecropper. In 1907, his relatives arranged for a young woman he had never met to travel to America to marry him. Clarence Nishizu was born to these parents in 1911.

Back in Napa, by 1914 elected officials were warning voters of a disaster for California's grape and wine industry if Prohibition became law. J.H. Wheeler joined other small farmers to form the Napa County Viticulture Protective Agency. By 1916, Prohibition proponents from the Anti-Saloon League bought advertising on Napa's electric train cars. When the California Grape Protective Associations condemned saloons, an outraged John Wheeler and other vintners withdrew from the association in protest. When

Prohibition passed in 1920, Mr. Wheeler was prepared to go into the grape juice business. But by 1923, he had changed his mind, ripped up his grapes and planted walnut trees.

Clarence Nishizu died at the age of ninety-five in 2006. He was a humanitarian, civic volunteer, philanthropist and advocate for Japanese Americans. *Courtesy of Kathy Tanaka.*

Clarence Nishizu remembers his parents' pilgrimage back to St. Helena. "In 1927, during the summer vacation after my sophomore year in Anaheim High School, my family went to Yosemite and, afterwards, to Napa County to see Mr. Wheeler." The Southern Pacific Railroad provided passenger service to Napa until 1929, so the trio likely would have traveled up from Los Angeles on the train. The family found Mr. Wheeler at home, and they were pleased when he recognized Mr. Nishizu. Son Clarence comments, "Mr. Wheeler was a kindly and considerate person, but he was very frugal in spite of his wealth."

Seventy years later, in 1991, when he was eighty years old, Clarence Nishizu and his wife, Helen, repeated the family pilgrimage, journeying one last time up valley:

> *We stopped at the old Wheeler house, which is over one hundred years old, and knocked at the door, but nobody was home. The stately mansion still stands like the day it was built with an ornate stone wall around the outside of the house. As I stood on the raised porch and looked through the window, I visualized eighty-five years ago when young Koheiji Fujino was working in that kitchen.*

The Nishizus wanted to find out what happened to Mr. Wheeler. They visited the St. Helena Grower's Foundation and spoke with the secretary, who recalled that her father had once worked for Mr. Wheeler. Raymond

Vineyards bought the property in 1974 and still operated a vineyard there in 2012. Clarence Nishizu concludes, "As I left the winery I recalled the story of the late night chicken supper that Mr. Taichiro Ueno told me twenty-five years ago."

Chicken Gohan

2¼ cup Japanese rice
¼ pound boneless chicken thigh, cut into small pieces
2 tablespoons soy sauce and 1 teaspoon soy sauce
¼ gobo (burdock root)
1 tablespoon sake
1 tablespoon mirin
½ teaspoon salt
3 inches carrot, peeled and cut into small and thin rectangles
4 shiitake mushrooms, stem removed and sliced thinly
¼ konnyaku, cut into small and thin rectangles and blanched

Wash Japanese rice and drain in a colander. Set aside for 30 minutes. Season the chicken with 1 teaspoon of soy sauce. Scrape off gobo skin and thinly shave into strips. Soak gobo srips in water for about 5 minutes. Drain the gobo. Put 2½ cup of water in a pan. Add sake, mirin, 2 tablespoons of soy sauce and salt. Heat the soup. Add chicken, carrot, gobo, shiitake and konnyaku in the soup and simmer for about 5 minutes, skimming off any foam or impurities that rise to the surface. Stop the heat and cool it off. Separate the simmered ingredients and the soup, using a colander. Add some water in the soup to make 2½ cup of liquid. Put washed rice in rice cooker and pour the liquid over the rice. Lightly stir and place simmered ingredients on the top. Start the rice cooker. When rice is cooked, let the rice steam for about 10 minutes before opening the lid. Mix the rice with rice spatula.

Clarence Nishizu moved from Los Angeles with his parents to Garden Grove in 1917. At twenty-one, he took over his father's debt-laden farm during the Depression. He was interned with his family during World War II. After internment, he campaigned for redress for internees. "He wanted to help unify and retain Japanese American culture," said his daughter, Carol Matsuoka, who was born at Heart Mountain internment camp in Wyoming after her parents were relocated there in 1943.

In 1962, Nishizu moved to Fullerton, where he was a prominent member of the Japanese American Citizens League. He also helped raise funds for construction of the Orange County Agricultural and Nikkei Heritage Museum at Cal State Fullerton, where he was awarded an honorary doctorate in 1999 for his leadership activities.

TIME PASSING IN NAPA

Only local and regional history satisfies the need to remember the most intimate matters, the things of childhood...the goods, machines and tools with which they worked, and the groups in which they were raised.
—Joseph Amato, Rethinking Home

One way to pour time through the hourglass of our lives is to read about Napa as it once was. Louis Ezettie, realtor and journalist, wrote several columns in 1961 that take us back to the past. If we listen to Napa's elders today, we can glean much from their memories. This essay intersperses Ezettie's memories (in italics) with the recollections of the Merry Mariners social group from the First Presbyterian Church (in quotes).

Sunday afternoon and a great crowd of baseball fans pours out to watch the great rivals, Napa and Vallejo, whose lineup included the mighty Ping Bodie for Vallejo and the slugging Lloyd Russell for Napa engaged in another thrilling contest. The bloomer girls' baseball team making a cross-country barnstorming trip and annually meeting a local men's aggregation...Employees at California Glove Company making up two baseball teams called the Giants, captained by Bill Simpkins, and Midgets, led by Archie Jacobsen, and meeting in the friendly combat as other employees formed rooting sections to cheer their favorite side.

"We grew up digging up arrowheads out on Old Soda Springs Road. There must have been a large Indian population here...My family even remembered hearing about a powwow in 1910."

Customers having dinner at Kunzel's Restaurant on the east side of Main Street near First, where a meal consisting of pearl barley soup, roast beef and potatoes, coffee, and homemade pie cost 25 cents, cooked on a woodstove...School children buying lunch put up in a bag for them at Levi Chapman's grocery, southeast corner First and Brown Streets, with the lunch items including chipped beef, cheese crackers, fig bars, and some kind of fruit for 15 cents. People waiting in line at Mason Bakery, southwest corner of Brown and Fourth Streets, to buy hot bread just out of the ovens at three loaves for 25 cents, and

GIRLS' ALL-SCHOOL TEAM

Coach Carter, Mgrs. Flanagan and Gibb
Zimmerman, Heston, Korf, Dittmer, Owen
Shaw, Captain Guidotti, Hammond

This team, captained by Muriel Guidotti and coached by Miss Carter, turned out to be the pride of the entire school. It was the first girls' team to undertake real outside competition, and it brought home a win from nearly every game.

It is to be hoped that the example of this team will lead to more extensive interscholastic contests for the girls.

The girls' basketball team at Napa High in 1912. *From the 1912* Napanee, *courtesy of Robert Northrup.*

Horses once drank from the river at Trancas Street, right near the Elks Lodge. *Courtesy of Napa County Historical Society.*

if you found a five dollar gold piece in your bread, it was not there by accident, as the owner put four or five gold pieces in different loaves to promote sales; and at Regli Brothers Bakery (Napa City Bakery) they gave 20 tickets for $1, each ticket good for one loaf as an inducement to the hotel and restaurant trade.

"We walked our cattle from Sonoma to Napa, and grazed them on the river behind what is now the Elks Club. Children would take turns watching the cattle."

Professor H.L. Gunn, head of the local business college, whose penmanship with its elaborate flourishes and delicate shading was a work of art…The big bell in the courthouse tower ringing out an alarm in the still of the night, and you consult your handy alarm location card distributed by and with the compliments of A.H. Smith insurance company, and if it's a downtown number, you might jump on your bicycle and hurry to the scene.

"Old town used to have a lot of boardinghouses…Do you know why there are Cupolas on downtown houses? They were 'widow's walks,' where wives watched for ships coming up the river after being out at sea."

The big fruit cannery on 4th street opposite the SP Depot burned to the ground, throwing many people out of work, and was never to be rebuilt. The Chinese vegetable garden and watermelon patch on Soscol Avenue, back of where the Gasser Motor Plant stands, which was often raided by kids living on the west side of the river, who

Napa Canning Company before it burned down, as described by Louis Ezettie. *Courtesy of Napa County Historical Society.*

Louis Ezettie. *Courtesy of Napa County Historical Society.*

would swim across, snatch melons, and then push them across the surface of the water as they made it back to shore.

"There were skating rinks all over town, on the top floor of the Hatt Building, and on Silverado Trail by Juarez. We all used to go to Patrick's [now Anette's] candy store afterwards."

The first talking motion picture shown in Napa was presented at the movie theatre located on the east side of Main Street between 3rd and 2nd streets, and Eddie Cantor was the featured actor…Julio Banchero, talented accordionist and expert billiardist, attracting music and dance lovers to Armory Hall (Migliavacca Building) and winning himself a long engagement as a solo accordionist on the Orpheum Pantages west coast vaudeville circuit. James J. Jeffries, World's Heavyweight Champion, spending several days in town when he came here to take a small part in the cast of a show headed by Bert Lytel and Evelyn Vaughn at the old Opera House. Tom Sullivan, a local vocalist, probably setting a record for the number of encores ever accorded a performer on a Napa stage, singing for the first time the very sentimental song entitled, "Honeyboy, I Hate to See You Leaving."

"I remember you from when I was a bookstore clerk at Napa College in the late '70s. You danced in the quad."

Once one of the great prune growing areas in the state, Napa County, had seen the industry give way to an almost complete turnover to grape growing. Sunsweet disposed of the packing and shipping departments on Jackson Street, and reduced their workforce from 100 to 25 people. Napa Valley grown prunes, in my estimation, surpassed the quality of the fruit grown in other parts of the state. Every year we kids earned enough money picking prunes at the Frank Bush Ranch near Little Trancas to pay for school clothes and schoolbooks.

Old Sunsweet building next to railroad tracks, Napa 2003. *Courtesy of Lauren Coodley.*

Chapter 3

THE 1920S

VOICES FROM EARLY BROWNS VALLEY

Ever since I saw a photograph of prune trees in Browns Valley, I longed to learn more about the area. What grows there reflects the lives of its inhabitants. Once upon a time, indigenous peoples came over the land bridge to North America. They migrated in waves beginning more than ten thousand years ago. Black oak acorns were their most important food crop. Men and women collected acorns together and stored them in specially built caches. Women dried, shelled, ground and leeched the nuts. They pounded shelled acorns in stone mortars made of igneous rock, stored them beside Napa Creek to remove the bitter tannin and used them in mush, soup and bread. They roasted bay nuts in their shells in hot ashes, ground them into flour and rolled them into small cakes. The berries of the toyon and madrone were the last harvest of the year. The people ate toyon berries after baking or roasting them in a basket of hot coals; they ate madrone berries raw or heated over hot coals. Manzanita berries could be eaten fresh or dried, made into a drink similar to apple cider or ground into flour for cakes. These plants are all still found in Browns Valley.

The lives of the indigenous people changed forever in 1821, when the Mexican government built what would be the last mission in Sonoma. General Mariano Vallejo led the Mexican army in dislocating the people he found here. He then offered the hills and valleys east of Sonoma to his friends, a group who named themselves Californios. Salvador Vallejo,

George L. Throne pear-spraying crew, 1911. *Courtesy of Diane Dillon.*

brother to Mariano, took the area that would later be called Browns Valley. In 1848, at the end of the war with Mexico, America gained much of the territory that had been Mexican, and Californio rights to landownership ended. American settlers from all parts of the country moved in to claim the land or to buy it. Almost everyone who had a land grant in the Napa Valley lost most of it. Salvador Vallejo sold some of his northern and central land to settlers, but John E. Brown claimed that he purchased Browns Valley for a horse and buggy.

By the 1880s, Mexican ownership of the Napa Valley had been almost forgotten. The new settlers came from all over America. One such settler was Diane Dillon's grandfather George Throne. His parents bought their property in Browns Valley in the early 1890s. By 1900, George's widowed mother, Lanora, was living in Napa with her five children. She died in 1904, when George was only nineteen years old. At that young age, Diane's grandfather began managing the prune farm, which was to the north of the once-famous Century Oak, located almost across the street from what is now Browns Valley Market.

In 1910, George married Ivy Hobson, who'd been raised on another farm on the north side of Redwood Road. Diane Dillon writes, "I have my grandfather George's dance card from a dance at the Browns Valley Farm Center…Ivy is his first and last dance." Diane's grandparents lost the farm to foreclosure during the Great Depression. She writes, "My mother would drive me when I was a child (or in her later years, have me drive her) out

First Street to Browns Valley Road, to pause and look at the Century Oak, and talk about the family farm."

Some people owned prune orchards in Browns Valley; others worked for them, picking fruit. Olamae Wade was three years old when a flood washed her family's house down a river in Texas. They journeyed to Napa in 1924, pitching a tent at Gardner's Auto Camp along Napa Creek downtown. In 1928, the Wades rented a farmhouse where prune orchards stretched "as far as you could see," as she described to me when I met her in 2003. The house is still standing on Browns Valley Road across from what is now Karen Drive.

There were also peach and almond orchards, owned by families that included the Hobsons, the Minahens and the Buhmans, which filled the area with pink and white blossoms in spring. Along with her mother, sisters and brothers, Olamae picked prunes. Eventually, Mrs. Mary Wade became a harvest captain for some of the ranches. After harvest, the children attended Browns Valley School, then a one-room school with eight grades and twenty-six students, who were kept warm by a wood-burning stove.

Although very few orchards remain, fruit continues to thrive in Browns Valley. By continuing to provide sustenance to its citizens, Browns Valley

Olamae Wade's mother with her prune harvest crew and employer, Mr. McKenzie. *Courtesy of Olamae Combellack.*

holds on to some of its history. In our recent book on Napa's farm history, Paula Amen Judah and I described the figs and quinces at Connelly Ranch and included Keigi Sugiyama's radiant persimmon and Fuji apple fruit trees. We were pleased to include this recipe from Dorothy Wurz, who still grows prunes at Wurz Ranch:

Fresh Prune Torte

Recipe from Jobyna Carpenter (sister-in-law of Dorothy Wurz)

Cream 1 cup sugar with ½ cup butter, plus 2 eggs. Sift together 1 cup flour, 1 teaspoon baking powder and a pinch of salt. Add together a little at a time. Fold in nuts (optional). Spray an 8- by 8-inch baking pan with Pam. It will be a thick batter. Use 24 halves of fresh prunes, pushing them down into batter, skin side up. Sprinkle with cinnamon and lemon juice. Bake 1 hour in a 350-degree oven.

In addition to the recipe for Prune Torte, *Napa Valley Farming* features local recipes for Pear Bread (Peggy Aaron) and Sour Cream Apple Pie (Loraine Geddes).

Elmer and Robert Bickford standing behind Connolly Ranch overlooking prune orchards in Browns Valley in 1911. *Courtesy of Robert Northrup.*

PART I

NAPA'S ROARING TWENTIES

What were the Roaring Twenties like in Napa? We can glimpse that time through the articles by journalist Jane Smith. She grew up at 1915 Second Street:

> *I learned to love the neighborhoods of old Napa during my long career as a piano student. On lesson days, I found the shadiest streets and learned where to swipe loquats, plums, and snapdragons. I knew who would be out on their front porches, from Mayor Oliver Hoffman to the ladies who sat outside all summer.*

Napans in the 1920s were fascinated by the Asylum, which was renamed Napa State Hospital in 1922. Jane Smith remembers her neighbor Abbey Halteman, who worked as a nurse there:

The Napa Asylum was renamed the Napa State Hospital in 1922. *Courtesy of Napa County Historical Society.*

> *She drove a sporty Ford and sat up high in the driver's seat, erect as a queen in her carriage. She wore her silver hair coiled in a bun on top of her head held by tortoise shell hairpins and her nurse's cap on top of her bun…I admired her beautiful working clothes, the long sleeved black and white striped uniform covered by a starched white apron, white shoes and the cap. She worked every day at the hospital, a turreted mysterious place where the corridors of the main building were hushed, where the floors shined with wax, and the waiting room was graced with green potted palms…the very picture of a place of rest and healing, but a madhouse nonetheless…People like Abbey Halteman were the guardian angels of the mad.*

Smith remembers the ballgames attended by Napa townspeople, where they watched the inmates play inside a fenced field. These inmates worked in the dairies and orchards. In 1923, Napa's prize-winning pears were canned, dried and shipped green. The biggest employer during the fruit-picking season was the Napa Fruit Company, which became famous for its "Napa Pack." In 1923, the *San Francisco Chronicle* noted, "A great bulk of prunes are dried in the sun, but of late years the dehydrator had come rapidly to the fore, and Napa becomes the third county in the state for the number of its dehydrators." Locally grown fruits and nuts (mainly prunes) were sold all over the country. William Fisher installed a fruit dryer on his property near Union Station at Trancas where other fruit growers would bring their stock.

Herman Baade, an agriculture teacher at Napa High School, helped to organize over a dozen centers where farmers met to share ideas. Napa County farm centers were in the following areas: Browns Valley, Los Carneros, Las Amigas, Coombsville, Salvador, Soscol and Oak Knoll, along with Rutherford Grange in Rutherford and the Tucker Farm Center in Calistoga. The *San Francisco Chronicle* reported, "These farm centers are also mediums for social interchange, 'getting acquainted' in a way that is pleasant and often produces life-long friendships…Newly arrived settlers will be interested in Mount George Farm Center in particular, because it is the 'daddy' of them all, having been the very first established in the United States."

These one-story buildings featured kitchens donated by farming families. Farm advisors oversaw the transition in Napa from grain, oats and pasture to horticulture and, eventually, to viticulture. 4-H was created during this period, out of concern for the isolation of rural children and to teach citizenship and leadership. Ruby Flowers, a home economist, was an early leader of the Women's Auxiliary to the Farm Centers, where women learned to cover lampshades, stuff mattresses and can with pressure cookers. These centers eventually became the Farm Bureau.

Many Napa residents looked back fondly to their lives in the fields and orchards in the '20s. Olamae Wade Combellack recalled skating down Browns Valley Road into downtown Napa without fear of being hit by cars. Rudolph Boysen, a farmer and amateur horticulturalist, invented the boysenberry in 1924 while living on Third Avenue. He combined pollen from a blackberry and "some other kind of berry." When he left for Anaheim in 1925, he took six vines with him, which he planted in an orange grove. His new berry was 50 percent bigger and juicier than the blackberry, but no one was interested until 1932, when a scientist from the U.S. Department of Agriculture came to Anaheim. The scientist found Walter Knott, who ran a berry truck garden. The two of them tracked Boysen down, who led them to the orange grove where the vines were half dead, on the verge of extinction. Out of those vines, Knott's Berry Farm was created.

The 1925 Napa High yearbook, the *Napanee*, describes what students were doing after graduation. Ruth Daly was teaching at John Shearer School, while Lois Daughty was "at home" in Napa, as was Wayne Douglas. Eugenia Donahue was employed at JC Penney's, Blanche Lui worked at La Mode Beauty Parlor and Verona Steere worked at the Napa Post Office, while Muriel Van Pelt was "Mrs. Kenneth Johnson" in

Postcard of Fuller Park, founded in 1905. *Courtesy of Mr. M.*

Vallejo. Barbara Chisholm was the assistant cashier at the Hippodrome Theater, and the Edwards sisters were both attending Napa Business College. Erler Frisch was at Keig Shoe Company, Lucille Wilson clerked at Woolworth's, David Wright worked for Abe Strauss and Robert Manasse worked for Sawyer Tanning Company.

The City of Napa had purchased ten acres of orchards in 1905 for $12,000. The land was cleared for the first city park, designed by J.H. Chalmers. In 1919, the park was renamed after Mayor Jack Fuller, who had presided over its purchase. Jane Smith, born in 1922, describes her birthday celebrations in Fuller Park:

> *I remember my peach Crepe De Chine dress, white silk stockings stationed by a garter just below the knee and black patent leather Mary Jane shoes, with button straps. Bangs trimmed for the occasion by Mr. Lui, at Lui's beauty shop in Main Street. Cake and candles and ice cream from Modern Dairy made the day. Presents, too. Writing paper for little ladies, pin the donkey on a tree.*

Jane recalls that there was only one policeman, and "he went home at night." Jane Smith and cousins Bob and Jackie would climb up the big cannon on the northeast corner of the park and shoot imaginary cannonballs at the motorists passing by on Jefferson Street:

> *Little did I know that I would have to say goodbye to Bob and Jackie many years too soon...but they loved me all their lives, and I them, and our bonds were forged forever from our young beginnings in Fuller Park, tramping in my Aunt Flo's Browns Valley orchard, and playing in the empty lot on Second Street, telling stories in the twilight.*

The 1920s may not have roared in Napa, but those who lived then remember those years as deep and rich and sweet, like the fruit that bloomed everywhere. Just before her death in 2001, Jane Smith visited the house on Second Street and found "ghosts still sitting in the chairs."

A TANNERY IN A TOWN, I AND II

I see it sometimes, and it could be under glass, a little museum of people and implements from another place and time. The Village and its life was taken from them, and it was given to me. I tried my best to return it.
—*John Baskin,* New Burlington: The Life and Death of an American Town

I

Once upon a time, seven wharves were constructed along the Napa waterfront, along with lumberyards and warehouses. Back then, steamers carried both agricultural and industrial products, sometimes transporting entire flocks and herds of livestock to our docks. French Albert Sawyer from New Hampshire was visiting Napa when he noticed that local butchers were discarding sheep pelts with wool still on them. He purchased a pile of those pelts and started a wool-pulling business on the banks of the Napa River, aided by Chinese laborers. Soon, he was curing hides, pickling them in brine and shipping them back east.

Some workers at Sawyer Tannery in 1899: Ah Chong, Chas Philips, Joe Ezettie, Robert Thompson, the Wilson brothers, Louie Cassayre Ezettie, August Manasse, George Thompson and Louis Banchero. *Courtesy of Napa County Historical Society.*

Fiftieth-anniversary celebration of Sawyer Tannery in 1919. *Courtesy of Napa County Historical Society.*

In 1870, he founded the Sawyer Tanning Company on South Coombs Street. A year later, French Sawyer invited Emmanuel Manasse, a German immigrant who was running a successful tannery in the Mission District of San Francisco, to move with his family to Napa to work for him. Manasse joined the company and rapidly developed new methods for tanning sheepskin and buckskin.

In 1900, the tannery was buying deerskins for thirty-eight cents a pound in the summer and in winter, for twenty-eight cents. Wet, salted cowhides cost nine cents a pound, and horse hides cost two dollars. By 1909, Sawyer Tannery had developed Napatan Waterproof Leather and Napa Patent Leather, and Emanuel Manasse became co-owner of the business. In 1917, Emanuel's son, Henry Manasse, opened a shoe store downtown and built a family home at 845 Jefferson Street, pictured in Tony Kilgallen's *Napa: An Architectural Walking Tour.* When the supply demands of World War I caused a shortage of chemicals, Sawyer sent engineers and miners into the surrounding hills and found chrome ore to make dichromate of soda, the chemical essential to tanning.

By the 1920s, Sawyer had become the first tannery west of Chicago to produce patent leather, and in 1927, it developed chromed tan leather (the ideal material for fashioning softball gloves) and, later, leather for baseball and welding gloves. In the '20s and '30s, the South Franklin neighborhood, a couple blocks from the tannery, was home to tanners, paper hangers, stevedores, river men and their families. Lin Weber sketches the scene:

> *Edna and Rita Guisti grew up in that neighborhood on Levee Street (now Riverside Drive). They went barefoot all summer, wearing ragged cotton dresses with bloomers underneath. They often climbed the big oak of Oak Street, which was by the water. It had a rope swing, on which they swung as high as possible before jumping off into the water... The river was still clear; carp would come to the surface, and children tried to spear them with willow branches to sell to Napa's remaining Chinese families.*
>
> *The big whistle on top of the water tower at the Sawyer Tannery was one of life's regulators for children like Edna and Rita, and for their parents, as well. It blew every day of every year at 6am, 12 Noon and 4pm.*

Even during the Depression, Sawyer Tannery continued to thrive, turning out woolen lining for coats and all kinds of gloves. The tannery offered hard work, sometimes dangerous and always involving exposure to the toxic materials used to tan hides. But a man could make a living with his hands throughout most of the twentieth century.

All of that began to change after the 1980s, when corporations were allowed by "free trade" agreements to move their operations out of our country. Napa factories shut down one by one. Rough Rider had closed its doors in 1976; Kaiser Steel, in 1983; and Sawyer Tannery gave final notice to its employees in 1990. With the clanging shut of the great doors, the leveling of the buildings and the transition of blue-collar workplaces to art galleries and tourist centers, scores of workers were displaced, and young high school graduates lost the opportunity to work at manufacturing jobs.

As historian Carol Kammen writes, "Local history is a process of learning, and it is about explaining causes—the how, and the why, of the past...the letters of a prominent family might be held in a local archive while the letters of a laborer in a tannery were not thought about or considered important enough to collect." What stories could the men in this photo tell us, and who will pass them on? Will their personal histories be lost or forgotten, left in shoeboxes and family scrapbooks?

II

In Part I, I wondered, "What stories could the men in this photo tell us, and who will pass them on?" My first answer was from Sharon Arnold: the picture of the Sawyer color wheel includes her father, Chester van Gorder, "the man on the right with the dark hair." Her mother "doesn't remember any stories other than it was hard/dirty work and that he didn't have set hours. He went in at 7:00 [a.m.] and worked until everything was done and many days that was early afternoon so he would fish the Napa River."

My next correspondent was Peter Manasse, who wrote: "I am the 4th generation and only tanner and Manasse left in this town. Emanuel Manasse was my great-grandfather." He told me that it all really began in 1869, when Sawyers used to cure hides with salt and send them to Chicago for tanning. His great-grandfather Manasse came up to Napa on horse and buggy "and said, 'Look I can tan those things.'" Emanuel's first house, built in 1886 at 443 Brown Street south of Oak, was known as the Manasse Mansion until recently, when it was renamed the Violet Mansion and awarded Historic Landmark status.

Sawyer color wheel workers, including Chester Van Gorder. *Courtesy of Napa County Historical Society.*

Peter Manasse confirmed that after his great-grandfather joined the Sawyer Company, he rapidly developed new methods for tanning sheepskin and buckskin. Emanuel's sons Ed, August and Irving began working at Sawyers. Ed stayed with the company, while August founded Manasse Block Tannery in Berkeley. Irving later founded his own tannery next door, CalNap, in 1945. Ed and his wife had four boys: Gerald, Robert, Phillip and Irving (Peter's father). The Edward Manasse House at 495 Coombs Street is also a registered Historic Landmark.

Mr. Manasse remembers the "whistle blowing every day at seven and one and four," the chemicals and dissolved hair being tossed into the Napa River while the fleshings went to a tallow company. He recalls the barges coming up the river bringing diesel fuel for their boiler and the hides arriving by freight train. He recollects driving a big flatbed truck across the Third Street Bridge to pick up the hides at the train depot at Fourth and Soscol. Sawyer Tannery was such a major employer that "most people did work at the tannery in high school or grammar school." Napa was so small that "if I drove my parents' car too fast downtown, a police officer would call them." Wayne Taylor sent me this description of his childhood near the tannery:

> *I lived on Pine Street and attended Shearer Elementary…The tannery was only a few blocks away. I recall going to a side door of the building on a warm summer day and getting free leather scraps from a kindly gentleman employee whose machine was close by. A leather scrap combined with rubber strap cut from an old auto inner tube formed the action (parts for a slingshot)! Of course, this all started with a forked piece of wood trimmed from a tree. Now we had a neat toy for free… Several of us neighborhood kids would then compete to see who had the best accuracy in hitting tin cans with our homemade slingshot.*

Originally, Sawyer made baseball gloves, which it sold to all major glove manufacturers. Throughout the early part of the 1900s, between 80 and 90 percent of leather was tanned in the United States. During both world wars and the Depression, tanneries prospered due to the constant demand for military and domestic leather products. As Pete Manasse recalls, after the Japanese got into the business around 1955, Sawyers was forced to switch to shoe leather. In 1961, Pete Manasse came home from the navy and worked at Sawyer's making shoe leather. Business remained stable until the late 1970s. The Leather Supply Company tells us:

> *Russia was at war with Afghanistan, the Ayatollah took over Iran (hence an embargo on African hairsheep), and Turkey chose not to export raw sheepskins. These countries supplied the fine raw material used to produce lightweight organ leather. Further, the efforts of the Environmental Protection Act caused many tanneries to close rather than invest in compliance measures.*

By 1980, half the shoes in America were imported. Every year after, another 10 percent were imported, and by 1990, 100 percent of shoes were imported from other countries. After researching Sawyer Tannery, I wrote:

> *But something*
> *was made, in that factory,*
> *at least a living, as well*
> *as hand and footwear, and*
> *if the big clock no longer*
> *rings, and if there are no rhythms*
> *here and nothing made, just*
> *time lost, spent, missing—*
> *They called it tanning.*

Chapter 4
The 1930s

Two Love Stories from Dunn Lee Manor

Composed of a singular set of objects, each home occupies space and anchors lifetimes in the same way a tuft of grass catches and holds particles of soil.
—*Joseph Amato,* Rethinking Home

On a hot night in July, I sat with the owner of Candlelight Inn, Sam Neft, along with the man who grew up within its walls, Nilan Kincaid. Nilan, born in 1931, brought us photographs of his childhood home along with his own memoir. We sat in the same corner of the kitchen where he once ate pancakes with parents Muriel and Ernest and his brother Gary. This is a tale of two love stories: Muriel and Ernest and then Nilan and Barbara.

In 1926, Ernest Kincaid delivered mail in the Italian part of town, Alta Heights. Muriel Dunn taught Latin and Spanish at Napa High School. She left that job to marry Ernest in 1929. Together, they designed and built a house at what became 2724 Browns Valley Road. Later, the right of way was named Easum Drive, Muriel's mother's maiden name. Like everywhere in Napa, there was an orchard of prune, walnut, peach and pear. A creek overflowed in winter and dried up in summer. Soon, there were steps down to the creek bank and grapevines, some strong enough to use as swings over the water. Ernest and Muriel planted a garden that produced potatoes, green beans, watermelons, cantaloupes and artichokes. The family grafted eleven varieties onto three apple trees. Nilan's personal favorite was Red Delicious. To the north, along the

Ernest Kincaid with sons Nilan and Gary, 1936. *Courtesy of Nilan Kincaid.*

creek, the family grew wheat and corn. "Sometimes," Nilan remembers, "Sunday breakfast would include pancakes or waffles made from freshly ground wheat or corn. What a treat! Very filling!"

Muriel Kincaid joined the French Club in town. She was also a member of the Eastern Star, while Ernest was a Mason. The magnificent post office on Second Street, built during the Roosevelt administration, celebrated the laying of its cornerstone on May 7, 1933. The Masons marched, drumming and singing, from the corner of Main and Pearl to the new building. The grandmaster of the Masons sealed a time capsule with the city directory and newspapers in a metal box in the stone. By 1935, Ernest Kincaid had been promoted to assistant postmaster.

Nilan Kincaid explained that before Napa had dial telephone service, Pacific Telephone employed operators "who, when the light for a particular line number flashed, would say 'Number Please.'" Residents outside city limits (to the west, these limits were just past Ornduff Street, now known as California Avenue) had farmer line service. Kincaid details, "Each phone circuit required two separate wires, suspended from telephone poles. Service to Dunn Lee Manor was 21F3, i.e., 3 rings…Each subscriber would get the operator by turning a hand crank and every subscriber powered his own phone with dry cell batteries, 3 inches in diameter and 6 inches tall."

Mr. Kincaid brought the family mail home himself, but Nilan haunted the post office daily, waiting for his ham radio license. Before getting his license, he became a short wave listener. In 1941, he listened to BBC, Radio Australia and Radio Japan. The Japanese broadcaster read prisoner-of-war messages written by Americans. Excited about the possibility of connecting these broadcasts to the real American families waiting for news of their loved ones, Nilan wrote to these family members—and many wrote back to him.

The family raised chickens during the war. Nilan remembers, "It fell to the boys in the family to feed and water the chickens, clean the droppings and collect and clean the eggs." Their father would estimate the size of the eggs and pay his sons the wholesale egg prices published in the *Napa Register*. Any eggs beyond family needs would sometimes be sold to the neighborhood store (now the 7-11 on Browns Valley Road). Nilan adds that the family also maintained "rabbit hutches that could accommodate 4 to maybe 6 of the critters…Not bad eating."

Mrs. Kincaid had household help during the war. Al Fong ran the Napa Grocery on Main Street. His sister had escaped from China during the Japanese invasion and joined her brother there. As a high school student, Amy Fong lived with the Kincaid family four nights a week and returned to stay with her brother on weekends.

In 1943, Ernest Kincaid hired the first female mail carrier on the West Coast, Leila Hansen. For a while, the Kincaids boarded her in their spare room until she was able to rent an apartment on 1218 Elm Street, right near Kiwanis Park. Nilan, then thirteen, biked over to visit Mrs. Hansen and her daughter Carol. He found Carol up in an oak tree with a neighbor named Barbara Rosebrook. He and Barbara would date all through high school, with only a brief breakup during which, Nilan says, "I felt like I was widowed."

Near the end of World War II, there were ten families on the Browns Valley 21F line. Nilan writes, "It is amazing that this writer was able to use 21F3 to have extended phone conversations with the young lady who was to be his bride for 54 years." Following the end of the war, copper was again available for telephone service, and one-by-one, Pacific Telephone took over the rural telephone companies. In its final days, the Browns Valley Telephone Company (BVTC) was down to four subscribers; E.L. Kincaid was president. Pacific Telephone removed the wire from the poles, and those who wanted part of it got it. The Kincaid family took two large rolls, each about five feet in diameter and at least five hundred feet long. "Useful for low band amateur radio antennas," comments Nilan Kincaid.

An upstairs room in Dunn Lee Manor hosted a variety of guests. One was the manager of the Napa office of Pacific Gas and Electric, Mr. Jack Williams, who lived in Calistoga. During the war, gas was rationed so Mr. Williams rented the bedroom at the far end of the upstairs hallway, four nights a week. When gas rationing ended in 1945, a woman who drove workers by bus to Mare Island rented the room. Nilan Kincaid recalls, "Still later, perhaps '51 or '52, said bedroom was rented to a student at Napa Junior College...Said student, who shall be called Rudy, only pretended to be a student. Upon his sudden departure it was discovered that certain items stored in a closet off the upper hallway had disappeared: pearl handled opera glasses and .25 caliber revolver, both having belonged to Muriel Kincaid."

Muriel and Ernest Kincaid in 1968. *Courtesy of Nilan Kincaid.*

Dunn Lee Manor. *Courtesy of Nilan Kincaid.*

Nilan and Barbara were married in December 1953. She worked at Mare Island while he studied electrical engineering at the University of California–Berkeley. They lived in Richmond next to the Southern Pacific tracks. Nilan accepted a job offer at Northrop Corporation in Hawthorne, near Los Angeles. He moved there with Barbara, and they raised a family.

By 1954, Ernest Kincaid had become postmaster, a position he held until his retirement in 1960. Throughout the '60s, Nilan Kincaid recalls, "When it would have been prudent for the owners to live their remaining years elsewhere, the property was listed for sale. Yet, the lady of the house did not want to leave her beloved Dunn Lee Manor. If a prospective buyer had children, she would tell them how dangerous the creek was for children. Even after the adjoining property to the west was sold, she asked those buyers to rescind the transaction; this they refused to do."

On the Fourth of July 1972, Nilan and Barbara arrived for a visit. That evening, Muriel Kincaid held her newest grandchild, Timothy, in her arms for the first time. Then that night, she passed away in her sleep. Her husband died three years later. By 1976, Dunn Lee Manor had sold for about $77,000.

Decades later, Nilan Kincaid visits Napa regularly. He always comes to Easum Drive. On one of these visits, he found some discarded items by the southwest corner of the house: "One was an old, leather suitcase, with an old name tag, reading E.L. Kincaid, Vallejo, Calif. 1922. That was joyfully retrieved!"

DISCOVERING RITA BORDWELL, I AND II

There are four ways to write a woman's life: the woman herself may tell it, in what she chooses to call an autobiography; she may tell it in what she chooses to call fiction; a biographer may write the woman's life in what is called a biography; or the woman may write her own life in advance of living it, unconsciously, and without recognizing or naming the process.
—*Carolyn Heilbrun,* Writing a Woman's Life

I

In the 1930s, life expectancy in America was fifty-eight years old for men and sixty-two for women. The average worker earned $1,368 per year, while 25 percent of them had no jobs at all. Milk cost fourteen cents a quart and bread, nine cents a loaf. As California's agricultural revenues plunged by $400 million after 1929, its rural areas became poverty stricken. Two of the state's chief products—tourism and specialty crops—made California

Rita Bordwell, about 1930. *Courtesy of Napa County Historical Society.*

particularly vulnerable. What happened in Napa? At the Napa County Historical Society, I was glad to find one article about that era, written by Rita Bordwell:

> *A friend of mine, a member of a union, rang me up one day and asked me if I would be interested in a position as secretary to the new business manager that the Central Labor and Building Trades expected to hire. He took me to the Labor Temple to meet them: Otis Brown, Carpenters; Earl McCall, Laborers; Earl Mack, Painters, Will O'Keefe, Plumbers, Will Gellinger, Lathers; Bob Findley, Electricians; and Washington Mannering, Garment Workers.*

Labor unions gained the right to organize when President Roosevelt signed the Wagner Act in 1935, which protects the rights of employees in the private sector to discuss organizing and workplace issues with co-workers, to engage in collective bargaining and to take part in strikes and other forms of protected activities. After decades of struggles by workers for fair treatment, finally they were able to successfully organize—despite the Depression—with the aid of this powerful legislation.

In 1938, the Napa Central Labor and Building Trades hired George Bobst, who had been a labor leader in both San Francisco and Vallejo, as its business manager. The first union office was on Pearl Street, in back of the Napa City Bakery. Bobst realized that larger quarters were needed. He surveyed the town and found the Prohibition Hall at Main and Vallejo Streets. The Carpenters Union, which had the most funds at the time, purchased the building, and later on the other unions paid their share. Bordwell describes the plight of jobless workers in Napa:

> *Mr. Bobst operated an apprentice school at night to assist the unskilled workers. He spent most of the time in the field, contacting employers and employees, looking for work…The unions were unable to hire more office help, so often Mr. Bobst and I came back to the office in the evenings and on weekends. Often we had to wait for our paychecks.*
>
> *John Steinbeck, when he wrote* Grapes of Wrath, *must have met some who came to Napa in broken down machines wired together, and in trucks with undernourished and sick little children. Mr. Bobst went to the Red Cross and begged funds and his wife Flossie made baby layettes for them. I will admit the local boys did try to keep their workers busy, Sawyer Tannery, the prune plants and fruit sheds…but the waiting room in the Labor Temple was filled with unemployed men and women*

> *Mrs. Otterson* [the longtime fire chief's wife] *had a kettle of beans and stew on the stove all the time to help feed those unfortunates. Union men's wives donated blankets and Mr. Bobst put cots in his rumpus room; other families camped in tents on jobsites. Work was so scarce and we had so many unemployed workers that we had to divide the work, giving each two days and Mr. Bobst would say, "Well that will give them bread."*

Bordwell explained that the Cameron Shirt Company, which opened in 1901, was the first union shop in town, turning out one hundred dozen work shirts a day. W.H. Cameron, a salesman for Levi Strauss in San Francisco, founded the company and brought a young cutter named Bert Gans to act as superintendent in 1901. Rita Bordwell, former secretary to the

Rita at age two in a pear orchard on Redwood Road. *Courtesy of Napa County Historical Society.*

Napa Central Labor Council, wrote, "I don't believe there ever was any superintendent that was as popular as Bert Gans. San Francisco requested his help to affiliate with the Shirtmakers Union. All joined, at the request of Messrs. Cameron and Gans." Historian Howard Zinn writes:

> *I saw what hadn't been told about labor history, what magnificent events had taken place, what struggles people had gone through, what sacrifices, what risks, what courage had been shown, what had been demonstrated about the possibilities of what human beings can do once they get together.*

When I looked in the folder for labor at the historical society and found Rita Bordwell's lone article, it fed my hunger to learn more about the labor history of Napa. I took a look at a cookbook from the 1930s with contributions from union members who included not only carpenters, garment workers and retail clerks but also bartenders, fruit dryers, barbers and grain processors, as well as musicians and distillery workers. I wanted also to learn about Rita Bordwell herself.

II

Most women born in the nineteenth century appeared in the newspaper only twice: upon marriage and upon death. Born in 1885 on the corner of Second and Randolph, Rita Harren Bordwell challenged the conventions about what women should do and be. Before writing her history of the labor movement in Napa, she wrote a history of the fire department and organized a firefighter museum to preserve that history. In response to my request for information about Bordwell, Lee Mitchell writes:

> *I'm a retired Battalion Chief from the Napa Fire Department, a docent and the Chairman of the Board of Directors of the Napa Firefighters Museum at 1201 Main Street. Many of us old timers knew Rita Bordwell. When I was first hired by the City of Napa in 1965 she used to stop by for a visit with the "fire laddies." She always had a story to tell and would remind us that her father was one of the original volunteer firefighters on the Pioneer Engine Company here in Napa in the late 1800s. We have a picture of her in one of our display cases at the museum. She was a very special lady to all of us who knew her.*

I visited the museum and admired her photograph. From retired captain Bob Foley, I learned that Rita Bordwell had written the first history of the Napa Fire Department, covering the years between 1859 and 1962. Captain Foley leafed through drawers and handed me that history. Reading it, I learned that her grandfather William Kennedy, who had sailed around South America to get to California, had been both deputy sheriff and prisoner guard for Napa County between 1879 and 1900. His marriage to Ann Hogan, who traveled here by covered wagon, was said to be the second on record at St. John's Catholic Church on Main Street.

Bordwell tells how in early Napa, before 1859, the only resources to fight fires were wells and pumps: "Women and girls pumped, men passed the buckets." In 1859, the first volunteer fire company was founded; by 1873, the Napa Hook and Ladder Company had been added. Bordwell describes the vaudeville shows held at Napa High to raise funds for the volunteers and the New Year's Balls held at the Opera House, where the Napa Band played until midnight, when they broke for refreshments and dancing until 5:00 a.m. He writes:

> *My father* [Charles Harren] *served between 1884 and 1886. He was injured by a falling burning wall and resigned at the request of Mother—but he never missed a fire as long as he lived. We have a picture of my father in his uniform holding the bugle which was used to call "the boys" together.*

Rita reports that when there was a fire, "everyone turned out" to watch the friendly competition between the different volunteer fire companies. She praises Henry and Ed Manasse of Sawyer Tannery, whose own firefighting organization, the Reliance Hose Company, "always offered assistance" to the town.

Finally, in 1907, Napa created its first paid fire department, and a new fire station was built in 1926 on First Street at the site of the old Central School. The fire chief and his family lived on the west side of the building; the boys stayed in the east. The chief's wife organized a sewing club to help the needy, and the fire station opened the first repair shop for children's toys. The crews distributed Christmas trees for the community from the station.

Captain Foley remembers how Rita Bordwell organized the museum: "She shamed the guys into getting their photos for us." In her own hand, she inscribed the names of all the firefighters on the backs of the 589 photographs she collected. Local historian Nancy Brennan reminds us of Rita's contributions:

> *If there was a major effort required for anything in Napa, it was likely someone would suggest "asking Rita" for help and most likely received*

it. Bordwell was secretary of the Napa Labor Temple for a decade, Fire Department historian, life-long member of the First United Methodist Church, and member of Order of Eastern Star, Keystone Chapter.

John Tuteur, former Fifth District supervisor, writes:

Rita Bordwell became famous as the "6th Supervisor" after her retirement. She attended almost every Board of Supervisors meeting and kept copious notes on everything. I, along with all of my fellow supervisors, attended her memorial service when she died in the mid-1970s.

Karen Schoenfeld adds:

Rita religiously attended Board of Supervisors meetings and I am sure there is still a plaque in her honor located behind the County Administration building on Third Street. At the time I first met her in the mid-60s she was a petite, elderly lady who would generally inquire, "Are my roses too red?" This was in reference to the rouge which was generally pretty heavy on the cheeks!

This correspondence makes us want to know more about Rita. How did she spend her evenings? What did she read? What movies mattered to her? Where did Rita shop and get her hair done? What could her diaries and letters tell us? Are there photographs of her home at 1568 Palmer Street? What meals did she cook in her own kitchen? Sharon Sanders believes the plaque honoring her is embedded in the concrete in the large common area between the Hall of Justice and the Criminal Court building, surrounded by deciduous trees.

The *Napa Register*'s obituary of February 22, 1975, read: "Napa County's ageless 'sixth Supervisor' Rita Harren Bordwell enjoyed a noteworthy 'career' in the Napa Valley as the wife of a contractor, secretary to labor organizations…and friend to many, a kind word on her lips for others every waking moment of the day."

Barely three months after Rita's death, on my first trip to Napa, I stood at a phone booth in front of the courthouse at Second and Coombs, a block away from her birthplace, looking for a place to rent. I would teach women's history for three decades at the community college before I learned about "Napa's Great Lady."

EVERY MEMORY A DOOR

Hey, there! Hoop-la! the circus is in town!
Have you seen the elephant? Have you seen the clown?
Have you seen the dappled horse gallop round the ring?
Have you seen the acrobats on the dizzy swing?
Have you seen the tumbling men tumble up and down?
Hoop-la! Hoop-la! the circus is in town!
—C. Michael James Dennis, "The Circus"

Every memory is a door into the past. Andrew Clerici offers this remembrance of being a child in Napa when the circus trains came to town:

> *I used to go to the Depot in the morning and wait for the train. They would unload and set up for the 2 o'clock show and then another show in the evening. They had a little parade of animals through town about noon to advertise that they were there. By eight in the morning they were gone…everything was clean and you could not tell they had ever been here.*

The depot was at Fourth and Soscol. The circus train would enter town on the tracks of the Napa Valley Rail Road (NVRR), built from the head of navigation (the farthest point above the head of a river that can be navigated by ships) in the Napa River in 1864. The route ran from Skaggs Island all the way to Calistoga. Freight trains would continue their runs into the 1980s.

In the '30s, businesses like the Napa Glove Company already employed hundreds of Napans when Julian Weidler brought Rough Rider north from San Francisco in 1936 and built his clothing factory on land between the river and the depot donated by the chamber of commerce. Raw materials were delivered by steamboat to the factory; fashioned into shirts, pants and skirts; loaded onto freight cars; and sent across the country.

Across the river, Sawyer Tannery developed new kinds of baseball and softball mitts. Wayne Taylor describes his childhood on Pine Street near the tannery:

> *Another summer memory that occurred near the tannery was watching the older kids pushing hand powered lawn mowers over the weeds on the vacant lot at Coombs and Elm. This preceded lively games of baseball with bats and balls all provided by the participating kids. Up Pine Street, and across from Shearer School was the little market where we could exchange*

> *scrounged soft drink bottles for penny candy. Most of us kids did not know there was a Depression on. We just accepted what we had as normal and made the most of it. Your article caused the recall of these pleasant carefree memories for me.*

In 1930, Dave Cavagnaro organized the first Italian-Catholic Federation convention, the firefighter parade and the "Circus Fans" organization.

Dave Cavagnaro leading a parade on horseback. *Courtesy of Napa County Historical Society.*

Cavagnaro, son of Italian immigrants, had arrived in Napa as a baby in 1883 and been fascinated with what he could see, hear and smell of the circus ever since Al Barnes and the elephants paraded past his front door in 1918. Alpheus George Barnes Stonehouse was born in Canada in 1862 and ran his circus until 1929. His elephant parade included ten Asian elephants, among them the bulls Tusko, Black Diamond and Vance. They must have been a magnificent sight as they were let off at the train depot and paraded through the quiet town.

When Cavagnaro married, he and his wife, Nellie, ran the Brooklyn Hotel at Third and Soscol, the gathering place for the Italian-American community. Dave tended bar, sang and played his concertina. He, Nellie and kids Anita, Ray and Robert lived upstairs; they rented rooms to single Italian men working on the railroad. We know that on April 18, 1935, Dave Cavagnaro hosted a dinner at his hotel for thirty-five performers from the Tom Mix Circus and Wild West Show.

What was the Tom Mix Circus? In 1933, "cowboy star" Tom Mix had begun touring with two Liberty horses and the Ward sisters' aerial act. By 1934, his circus traveled with a cast of up to fifty performers, including a twelve-piece band. Some of them came here for dinner. In 1938, in the middle of the Great Depression, the Tom Mix Circus folded. That year, Dave Cavagnaro was fifty-eight years old. He decided to set aside twelve weeks of every year to travel with either Ringling Brothers or the Clyde Beatty Circus. Martin Mini writes about this family member:

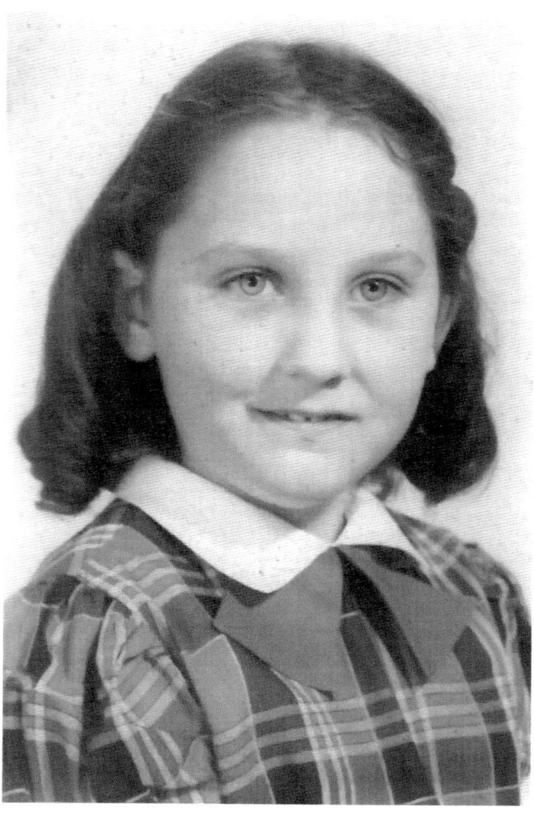

Cathy Mathews, age eight, 1956. *Courtesy of Cathy Mathews.*

He pitched hay, ran errands, helped in the front office, sold tickets, collected tickets, unloaded animals, set up and tore down tents, carried water to the animals...acted as a booking agent, functioned as an advance man and a roustabout.

The Ringling Brothers Circus began by traveling from town to town in small caravans led by animals, until it became so large that a train was needed. Despite the travel restrictions of World War II, President Roosevelt made a special declaration that allowed circuses to use the rail system. At age eighteen, Clyde Beatty left the family farm in Ohio on a one-day visit to see a real circus. In 1921, he left his life on the farm and began working for the circus as an animal groom. By his second year on the road, Clyde had been assigned a small polar bear act to train for the show. Acclaimed for his expertise with animals, by 1944 he had formed his own Clyde Beatty Circus.

In 1955, Dave Cavagnero lost his wife, Nellie. That year, Cathy Mathews was six years old, and her mother, Lucille, brought her to see the Clyde Beatty Circus at the Napa Fairgrounds. Cathy remembers, "The smells of sawdust, peanuts and popcorn. The trapeze artists came out in those big

NAPA COUNTY RECORD — Napa, California — August 5, 1959—Page 7

Come To The Napa Town & Country FAIR

AUGUST 13-16

EVERY DAY

FLOWER AND GARDEN SHOW — LIVESTOCK — POULTRY — AGRICULTURE HOME ECONOMICS — ARTS AND CRAFTS — INDUSTRY — COMMERCIAL EXHIBITS — F. F. A. — 4-H CLUBS — TALENT SHOWS, PROFESSIONAL AND AMATEUR — BANDS — ENTERTAINMENT — CLOWNS — CIRCUS.

AFTERNOON AND EVENING -- ALL FREE

THURSDAY, AUGUST 13 FREE KIDS' DAY

Kids' Day Parade and Picnic — 12 Noon.

John Strong Circus — Afternoon and Evening—Sponsored by the Napa Central Labor Council.

Band Concert — Veterans Home Band—2 p. m.

GRANDSTAND — VARIETY AND VAUDEVILLE SHOW — 8 P. M.

SPECIAL ATTRACTION — Bill Lorenz, the Mr. Pastry of the Ed Sullivan Show, and James Bream, imitating Mr. Pastry.

Ad for the Napa Fair in *Napa County Record*, August 5, 1959. *Courtesy of Napa County Historical Society.*

showy costumes—I was very impressed. Clyde Beatty had this whip that he snapped in the air at the lions and tigers." Dave Cavagnero must have been working backstage, and Andrew Clerici might have brought his own children to the Big Top that day.

All of these people were alive here, together, in the '50s, in a town that was by then home to fourteen thousand souls, some of them surviving long enough to find their names in this very story. Images from the 1956 Clyde Beatty Circus can be viewed at www.beattycircus.com. Ringling Brothers performs once a year in Oakland or Sacramento.

Chapter 5

The 1940s

Listening for Trains

And if your room, restless one,
Is much too still, listen to the clatter
Of the freight, rattling past trestles
On the cool night breeze. Then follow
The moon to the side of the tracks,
Where the train is a long, slow dream
You can jump on.
—Peter Schmitt, "For a Sleepless Child"

Paula Amen Judah discovered this poem, adding:

> *When I was a little girl in Napa, living on Summit, and later Hoffman Avenues, I would do exactly as the poet advises. When the train came through in the night, my whole being shifted at the sound of the approach. I traveled with it, imagining that I was going somewhere wonderful, at the same time puzzling over the pit of yearning that overtook me whenever I heard that long whistle and steady respiration. Train sounds illuminated the natural loneliness I felt as a child, but the light was warm. I believed the train and I shared a secret about life that no one else knew.*

Napa, looking up Third Street from Alta Heights. *Courtesy of Mr. M.*

Peter Schmitt's poem and Paula's memory evoked this essay. When I first moved to Napa in 1975, thousands of people worked at the state hospital, as did I. I learned that in the old days, the patients would take the trolley up Soscol into downtown Napa, and old-timers told me that the tracks were buried when they built Highway 29. The only vestige was the Greyhound bus stop across from the gate to the Asylum (as the hospital was originally called). It was a quarter of a century before I learned more of the story of the trains.

Sam Brannan had been a Mormon, next a vigilante and finally an entrepreneur. In 1862, after visiting the spas of Europe, he decided to set up one of his own. He opened his spa around 1865 and named the town Calistoga. Brannan wanted people from San Francisco to be able to travel to his spa after they got off the steamboat at Napa Junction, so he and Nathan Coombs opened a stagecoach line. Coombs and Brannan's coaches, drawn by six horses, met passengers stepping off their steamboat at Suscol House Hotel and swept them up to Calistoga.

Brannan also wanted a railroad to transport his visitors, and he persuaded the state legislature to propose bonds for one. The first engine, called the Calistoga, arrived in Napa in 1865. In 1866, the Napa Valley Rail Road (NVRR) was built, with track laid down from North Suscol southward to connect with the California Pacific Railroad at Napa Junction. The switching yard for the trains was constructed in American Canyon, which is why it was named Napa Junction. Only a few miles from the first naval base on the Pacific Coast (Mare Island), trains were switched for Solano, Sacramento, Sonoma, Marin and the East Bay.

A traveler could board the train at Suscol; get off at Thompson Station, the Napa Depot at Suscol and Fourth Street or the West Napa Depot on California Street. Service to Calistoga was completed by 1868. Forests were felled on the hillsides to supply the wood-burning furnaces on the trains. California Pacific purchased the NVRR in 1869; Southern Pacific bought Cal-Pacific in 1885 and operated passenger service to Calistoga until 1929. In 1885, the Southern Pacific Railroad Company purchased the line and operated it for the next 102 years.

In 1905, when the electricity was connected for interurban train operation, Napa's mayor, J.A. Fuller, announced, "Napa for half a century has been slumbering in a Rip Van Winkle sleep but she has awakened at last." A great banquet was held by the 20,000 Club of Vallejo to celebrate the link between the Vallejo ferry and the railroad, which was located next to the ferry building. Businessmen feasted on oysters, peeled tomatoes and mayonnaise, sweet bread patties, French peas, desserts, cheese, coffee and

Napa Valley Railroad electric train at the depot in 1906. *Courtesy of Napa County Historical Society.*

Havana cigars. The first chartered electric train carried fifty-five officers and sailors from Mare Island to Napa, along with "several ladies and a ten piece band." The band gave a public concert at the Napa Courthouse. By 1907, the Napa-Vallejo and Benicia Railroad offered a special roundtrip for Vallejo women who worked at the canning company in East Napa; tickets were fifteen cents.

In 1929, the Southern Pacific shut down its Napa passenger line, cut river service from South Vallejo to Napa Junction and turned over mail delivery to the electric railroad. In 1930, Greyhound Bus Lines sought permission from the Railroad Commission to merge its companies in California to compete with the railroads. The Napa City Council, the Napa Chamber of Commerce and the Napa Central Labor Council opposed the expansion of Greyhound. They believed that the Interurban "had long rendered adequate, dependable, and comfortable transportation service," writes Ira Swett, railroad historian. But the Railroad Commission decided in favor of Greyhound. Worse events were in store.

In 1932, a fire erupted in Napa's electric train barn. Cars were destroyed, the expensive electrical equipment was incinerated and the railway seemed done. Manager Clyde Brown had to lay off all seventy employees, but townspeople came to the support of the Interurban, aggressively campaigning to get the big trains back in service. Feature ads were purchased in the newspapers calling for electric railway service to resume. None of these efforts saved the railway, and by 1938, buses had successfully replaced the electric train. During the 1930s, the building of the Bay and Golden Gate Bridges destroyed the financial success of ferry business. People no longer traveled from the East Bay or San Francisco by ferry to Vallejo and on to the electric train to Napa. Don Meehan wrote the following letter to the editor, remembering the old car tracks buried at Third and Jefferson Streets:

> *I used to march on them every fair parade during the Fifties and Sixties… There are only two Napa Interurban cars still in existence at the Western Railway Museum located on Highway 12 at Suisun City. I am a volunteer at the museum. Please drop by some weekend and say hello and look over some of Napa's history.*

Adding to Napa's railroad history, Mary Campbell wrote to me:

> *My family moved to Napa in 1947. My father was the Signal Maintainer for the Southern Pacific Railroad. We lived in the house for 14 years at 801*

8th street. I remember the steam trains sitting alongside the house and the water running down the street, also the Clyde Beatty circus in the summer and the elephants being unloaded at the junction of the tracks at Soscol Avenue. My father was the last Signal Maintainer to live in the house.

In 1987, the Southern Pacific Railroad was sold to the Napa Valley Wine Train, Inc. The new owner refurbished the cars to give visitors an opportunity to experience the romance of the past by cruising through the valley. Unfortunately, there is no way to travel up and down the valley to actually get anywhere. But we still get to listen to the sound of the train whistle; no doubt, many children in Napa travel with it in their imaginations, just like Paula did when she was a child.

FOLLOWING THE TRAIL

O bees, sweet bees! I said: that nearest field
Is shining white with fragrant immortelles.
Fly swiftly there and drain those honey wells.
—Helen Hunt Jackson, "My Bees"

I first met Wash Mannering through his obituary. I read that he had quit his job as a fabric worker at Cameron Shirt to open the Fitch Grocery Store, which he operated with his wife at the corner of Oak and Seymour, the corner where I once pushed my daughter in a baby carriage. Mannering had been a member of the Garment Workers Union and served as secretary and president of the Napa Labor Council. He was a member of the state Grange; he and his wife, Marian, worked at the monthly pancake breakfasts at the Grange Hall on Hagen Road.

When I knocked on beekeeper Swede Johnson's door on Spencer Street, I did not suspect that I would learn more about Wash Mannering. Swede's wife, Rena, knew Wash Mannering because her first husband, Winston Tennant, was Wash's friend from Napa High School, where Mannering was a member of an undefeated championship football team. When he married Marian Cooley in 1937, the wedding announcement described how "her long veil of tulle extended over the train of her frock and fell from a halo of stiffened tulle edged with orange blossoms." In 1941, the Mannerings bought the grocery store at the corner of Oak and Seymour. Rena comments, "It

Wash and Marian Mannering in front of their grocery store. *Courtesy of Barbara Mannering*

was a two-story house, and they lived on the top floor. Wash worked cutting shirts at Cameron Shirt Company, great big stacks of them, while his wife ran the store. She helped lots of people during the Depression, letting them pay on credit—how they did it, I don't know." Ken Munk, nephew of Wash Mannering, sent a favorite picture and wrote:

> *The photo shows both of them standing out front of "the store," when I was the stock boy stocking shelves. I always liked to hear Uncle Wash call me to me from behind the butcher counter with a hearty, "Hey K Munk" whenever I would show up. The old-timers who may have worked at Cameron Shirt Factory came to "the store" for homemade sandwiches made by Aunt Marian and her sisters in the kitchen behind the store.*

Obediah "Swede" Johnson worked in the Civilian Conservation Corps in Montana and California during the Depression. He arrived in Napa on a rail car around 1938, with twenty-five cents in his pocket, stopped at the depot and bought a doughnut and a cup of coffee for fifteen cents and headed for Lake County to work in the quicksilver mines. When World War II began, Basalt Rock Company built a complete shipyard on its property, and Swede Johnson was hired as a boilermaker. "I had never seen a ship, except in pictures," says Swede. Swede worked at Basalt Rock Company for thirty-eight years, retiring as the superintendent of the fabrication shop. "The union made the blue-collar people powerful. I don't think we'd have a pension plan without one," he told me.

Swede Johnson at home on Spencer Street, 2006. *Courtesy of Lauren Coodley.*

For forty years, Swede has raised bees and made honey and hasn't needed allergy treatment. Originally, Swede's hives were at Spencer and E Streets, where he lived for thirty years and kept up to twelve hives. Now he had five hives, which produced forty-eight quarts of honey in 2006, when I did this interview. One of those quarts of honey that I took home was the finest I've ever tasted.

Swede and his wife, Lillian, would square dance with Winston and Rena Tenant at the Grange Hall on Hagen Road. Rena had lived on Hermosa Drive for fifty-one years, where she had a third of an acre and raised a half dozen fruit and pecan trees. She "canned everything I could get my hands on," she says. Her cinnamon rolls were particularly memorable. Rena had a pet squirrel monkey named Shorty: "Salvador School children would come over on field trips to watch him ride on top of our dog's back."

After both lost their first spouses, Pastor John Fernandes married Swede and Rena on his son's land on Second Avenue. Swede and Rena describe with nostalgia a "little town" that ended at Jefferson and Trancas, at the airport. There were no hotels, and "I used to go downtown and know everybody," says Rena wistfully. They describe the disappearance of the dairies and the Chinese markets, one at the present site of Albertson's on California Street and another at the Learning Faire site on Main Street.

Rena Tennant-Johnson, 2009. Rena rescued this dog and named her Dolly. They grew so close that they both died within days of each other. *Courtesy of Jana Martinez.*

Rena has been a member of a women's group for sixty-seven years. The group originally met at First Baptist Church during the war, "when we all were pregnant—Marian Mannering already had her twin girls." The group called itself "The Club." During the war, the women rolled bandages at the Hospitality House on Main Street; during the '50s, they met at 8:00 p.m., after the kids were in bed, and "our husbands babysat." Fifty years later, "we still meet twice a month at Sizzler." Marian Mannering was also in a club for fifty years: the Friendship Club at First Baptist Church.

The devotion to work and family lived by people like Wash and Marian Mannering and Swede and Rena Johnson has not been noted by official histories. My interest and respect for them is what makes "doing local history" so endlessly fascinating. The Mannerings retired from running their grocery store in 1971, and Wash Mannering died in 1982. Marian Mannering outlived her husband for several decades, during which time she owned Marian's Dress Shop in the Food City Shopping Center. She passed away in 2003.

Rena and Swede Johnson celebrated their wedding anniversary on May 5, 2007. Rena Tennant-Johnson died in her home on Spencer Street on July 18, 2010. Swede Johnson died surrounded by his children on January 17, 2012.

Part I

The Construction of History, I and II

Farmyards were stages for concerts of sound. Doors squeaked and slammed. Boards were sawed and hammered. Boots made great sucking sounds when pulled out of the mud. Sweeping was a snare drum, raising clouds of dust. Rocks were broken and foundations were poured. Restive horses whinnied and neighed, cows bellowed…all the while the clinking and sucking pump filled buckets with splashing and swirling water.

—*Joseph Amato,* Rethinking Home

I

How is history constructed? All we have to help us understand the past are the traces that people leave behind: a rusting tractor, a quilt glowing with color, a Corona typewriter or a Magnavox record player. From these traces—which are all around us—we can try to imagine what came before.

One such box of traces was handed to me several months ago. Deb Jachens rescued it from a barn; it bore the marks of many rainstorms, some pages too mildewed to read. Librarian Stephanie Grohs and I sifted through layers and layers of crumbling papers to find the farm records of one man, Henry Luhmann. He was an egg farmer who invented a particular kind of brooder; his patent slip was in the box along with numerous guidebooks for raising poultry and receipts for eggs he shipped to San Francisco by steamer as early as 1926. There were only three photographs in the box. The first is inscribed, "Building a garage for the Platts; on left, wife Bernardine; on right, Ally Platt." The second is of Bernadine with her dog; in the third, she is pictured with farm manager George Nichols. How we longed for a story to go with the photographs!

Mrs. Beatrice Luhmann and farm manager George Nichol. *Courtesy of Deb Jachens.*

We do know this about Henry Luhmann: he was not only an egg farmer and a

Henry and Beatrice Luhmann, around 1940. *Courtesy of Deb Jachens.*

husband but also a leader in the community of farmers that came together during World War II. In the box were carefully typed minutes from a farm labor committee that he chaired. The minutes for the first meeting on April 24, 1943, noted, "The committee asked Mr. Henry Luhmann and others to interview Mr. Owen Duffy regarding the use of the buildings at the Napa State Farm for housing seasonal labor."

At another meeting on June 17, Henry Luhmann explained the progress made in securing housing facilities at the Silverado Farm Labor camp:

> *Andrew Fagiani suggested that part of the camp at Yountville be set aside for family groups…The chairman stated that Mr. D.B. Parker had offered to give Napa County a building located at the Stockton Japanese relocation center. Herman Baade offered to take the Monticello committee to Stockton to look over the building…Will Gosling submitted data about the production of Berryessa Valley in 1943: nearly 3000 tons of hay;*

> *about a thousand tons of grapes; 700 tons of dried prunes; 1000 tons of pears; 90 tons of plums; almost 4000 tons of grain; almost 7000 head of cattle; 2000 head of sheep; 3000 head of hogs; all of this entailing about 45,000 "man hours." The period of harvest was August 15–October 15; 150 laborers needed.*

This information about the Berryessa Valley is especially poignant since it would all be destroyed with the building of the dam in 1957. The committee met on May 13, 1944:

> *Mr. Fruehauf, treasurer of the Napa Valley Farm Labor Association and a member of this committee, stated that there are now working on the ranches, 78 Mexican nationals, and that there will be 492 working in this county at the peak of the harvest season…the labor shortage in Napa County is more critical than that in many other parts of the state, and therefore a special effort must be made at once to provide housing for harvest help if a portion of the crops now in prospect are not to be lost.*

Later that month, "it was agreed that the District Fair would put up a building. The state would try to supply cots, mattresses and blankets, housing 150 persons at the Fairgrounds. The committee asked for a 500 man camp to be established at the Silverado Farm Labor Camp at the State Farm at Yountville."

Six months later, in June 1945, a new dilemma emerged for the committee. Clyde Casady, secretary of Napa Valley Farm Labor Corporation, wrote to Mr. Luhmann asking him to "lend every effort possible in helping us solve the problem of security measures at the Silverado Trail camp. This camp is to be used to house German prisoners-of-war…The prune and grape crops…look to have the greatest tonnage to be harvested in the history of the valley…With a definite shortage in Mexican nationals, the only other source of labor available is prisoners of war."

In July 1945, the minutes of the Farm Council reveal an interest in the wartime temporary housing:

> *The committee urges the state to take all possible steps for bona fide farmers of the state to acquire such of these facilities as are needed for housing of themselves and/or personnel working on their farms…members of the Armed forces during the War should have the first opportunity to obtain units of these facilities for housing themselves and their immediate*

> *families* [and] *the farmers of the state be given the next opportunity to acquire the units.*

That same month Henry Luhmann wrote to Dr. Theo Miller of the Napa State Hospital to say that the farm labor committee had been advised of the "splendid help the patients have been in past years in our harvest… We were also advised that you have again granted permission to certain patients to aid in our harvest again this year. Indications are that we will have a very heavy crop of prunes and tomatoes and every person who is able and willing to help with this harvest will find employment."

In April 1946, Henry Luhmann recorded "the amount of foreign labor in the county last year, reaching a peak of 345 Mexican nationals in July and a peak of 645 foreign laborers in August, including Prisoners of War and Jamaicans." In July 1946, Luhmann was able to write triumphantly, "There have been allocated to Napa County seven steel barrack buildings: portable, prefabricated, angle frames, insulated, two doors, sixteen windows without partition, equipment of plumbing. Size 20 x 48″…It will be the duty of the committee to select the first seven growers to whom the offer to purchase shall be made." A week later, his last letter from this box is to W.D. Butler. It reads, "According to the decision of the committee, a notice has been put in the *Napa Register* giving all farmer veterans a chance to purchase surplus housing allotted to Napa County…Please be present and assist in allocating these buildings."

We can only imagine the emotion behind these letters, as well as the conflicts that undoubtedly occurred behind closed doors over the complex challenge of harvesting Napa's crops in wartime. Surely, other farmers recorded their own impressions of these discussions. Did any of the state hospital patients or prisoners of war write letters or diaries about being here in the 1940s? What about the groups described as Mexican nationals and Jamaicans? What did they tell their families about their experiences in this luscious valley? We do know that, until very recently, Napa was dotted with the Quonset huts built during the war and that state hospital patients were prevented from helping with the harvest after the '50s, when drugs replaced vocational therapy.

For all we know, there are a hundred things we don't know. Yet because someone saved these minutes, we know a little bit about the official business of growing crops during World War II. We don't know what Bernadine Luhmann was doing during that period at the family farm on 2275 Big Ranch Road. Perhaps she has neighbors, relatives or friends who can help fill out the picture. All history is a mixture of official sources and private memories. Every document saved is a gift to the future, and for that we can be grateful to Henry Luhmann for typing his minutes and to Deb Jachens for discovering this box of records and salvaging them.

II

Earlier, I wrote about the challenge of finding the story behind a box of artifacts given me. It contained receipts for egg sales, meetings of farm labor minutes and a few photographs with obscure handwritten notes on the back. I asked the public to help me identify those pictured. Marilyn Grover responded. As a close friend of Beatrice Luhmann, she was uniquely able to paint a word picture of this Napa pioneer. The two women met in 1972, when Luhmann was already eighty-one years old.

Beatrice and Henry Luhmann had traveled by covered wagon in 1913 to Napa and "pitched their tent downtown," until they earned enough to buy the farm on Big Ranch Road. They lived their whole lives on that farm. Marilyn commented, "Her marriage was tough, life was hard." Beatrice Luhmann wrote, "My upbringing was never buy anything you don't need if you owe money. We had a mortgage with crop failures and low prices for poultry." The neighbors' friendship began when Beatrice came calling on behalf of her church, St. Mary's Episcopal. As the friendship developed, Marilyn, who lived at the end of Soscol, would bike over to visit. Beatrice told Marilyn how she used to gather up the neighborhood kids and carry them to Sunday school in a wagon along the dirt trail of Big Ranch Road, "always getting more kids to come along." She also gave Marilyn a handwritten story about her discovery of a cross from the original church, a rare document of one woman's life:

> *Planted a young orchard of prune trees, while we were waiting for fruit went into the chicken business. The babies survived that meant more chickens… To make ends meet we raised fryers, the whole sale price was so low we dress them, price 20 cents a pound…* [illegible] *for the pan and delivered, that was my job, at the crack of dawn would get dressed from 1 to 3 in the morning and deliver in the afternoon.*
>
> *Now the cross enters. A Mr. Jordan living on Calistoga Ave. whose business was buying old houses wreaking them and selling the lumber. He bought our lovely old St. Mary's church. Underneath the stage was*

Poster, "Some New Poultry Wrinkle." *Courtesy of Deb Jachens.*

a catchall for junk. He found the old cross all broken in pieces. One day his wife ordered some fryers. He came to the door. He asked me if I taught Sunday school at St Mary's. I said yes. He says, "Come with me, I have something you should have." Went down in the basement, on the wall was hanging a cross. He told me where he found it and spent a lot of time fixing it. I thought he was going to give it to me. How wrong I was.

He told me that was how he made his living and it would cost me five dollars, a lot of money to spend on something I loved but did not need. One Sunday morning at Sunday school, I told Mrs. York about the old cross. She was the superintendent of the Sunday school. She said, "Don't worry. Connie, one of the workers on the altar guild, she will get it." They both belonged to the same lodge. I waited a long time, one day I asked. She said Connie had no luck. A few weeks after, Mrs. Jorden ordered more chicken. Mr. Jorden came to the door; I asked if he had the cross. He said, "You can have it for $4.50"...just about as bad as $5. This went on for over two years, every time it was 50 cents less. One day I saw him walking in town with a cane, barely able to move. It flashed into my mind if something happens to him, the dear old cross will be lost to us. Soon after, Mrs. Jorden ordered more chicken as usual. He came to the door. I asked about the cross, price $2.50. I said, "Sold at last"—it was safe.

At the time Marilyn met her, Beatrice still tended her garden and fruit trees. She also "grew beautiful orchids to give away," as well as gourds. Marilyn Grover remembers, "I had never seen such large gourds." Beatrice used a special drying process for her figs, and she kept boxes of feathers from her chickens, separated carefully by colors. With those feathers, she decorated hats.

Marilyn and Beatrice took drives around the valley together, an experience Marilyn loved because "she knew everyone, and could point out much of what you were looking at." In her last years, she had a dog, MacGregor, that "wouldn't let me near her bed" when she became ill. She died within a few days of her illness, working on the farm right up to the end; she was "energetic, animated, and generous." Marilyn's last act of friendship was arranging her friend's funeral. Out front of the farm was a thick plank painted with the letters "Luhmann"; Marilyn herself repainted the sign. It is still there, the old name covered with the name of the new residents, JK Farm.

Beatrice Luhmann (1897–1978) is buried in the family plot at Tulocay with her husband, Henry (1883–1972). Also buried there are two of their three sons and George Nichols (1884–1979). Who was George Nichols? I wondered in my earlier essay. Marilyn Grover knew the answer: "He had done the chores around the farm, feeding chickens, always pushing a broom around. Had a railroad pension…lived at a little place on their farm." When Beatrice died, Nichols had nowhere to live, and Marilyn became his conservator. Beatrice left her beautiful silver service to the church before she died, and the cross she treasured is still displayed in the lobby of St. Mary's on Third Street.

Prelude to Part II

Let's take a walk through Napa in the 1950s, when Stornetta's Dairy delivered milk and Colonial Bakery brought fresh-baked loaves of white bread and glazed doughnuts to every door. Teenagers gathered at Kenny's Drive-In on Jefferson or at the Wright Spot on Soscol and sometimes the KVON drive-in theater on Foster Road. They danced to live bands at the fairgrounds, bowled at Napa Bowl or Bel Aire Bowl, skated at the rink on Juarez Street. And they played ball, not only Little League, but also girls' softball. Under the leadership of their coach and manager, Ernie Collicutt, the Napa Shamrocks reached national prominence. Their pitcher, Carole Nelson, established an all-American record in 1955. Collicutt, who also led the Bartenders, Waiters and Waitresses Union, helped to create Kiwanis Girls Softball Field on Coombs Street, still going strong today.

You could buy baseball or softball gloves at Brewsters on the corner of Main and Pearl Streets. Its co-owner, Rachel Friedman, is described in "Mrs. Brewster's Double Life." If you needed your pants shortened, you would go to Cervone's Taylor Shop on Second Street. Nick Cervone immigrated to the United States with his father in 1949. When the boat entered San Francisco Harbor, the Golden Gate Bridge reminded him of the harbor at Naples, while the vineyards also reminded him of Italy. In 1955, the Cervones opened their tailor shop on Second Street in Napa, where Mr. Cervone continues to sew while opera music soars from the radio.

If you had a craving for won ton soup, you could find it at the Asia Café run by the Soon family. Eng (Sophia) Ching met her husband, Bing Soon, when he returned to China after serving with the American Air Corps during World War II. In 1948, they moved to Brown Street in Napa and joined Napa's small Chinese community of restaurant workers, shopkeepers, laundry workers and laborers. In 1959, they opened the Asia Café, where son Michael began as a greeter at the age of two. At home, Sophia harvested sugarcane from her backyard twice a year.

What if you wanted to buy perfume for a special occasion? You could walk down Jefferson to Family Drug, owned by Mary Anne Doud. Doud was one of only six women to graduate from the University of California Pharmacy College, and her proud family would visit her in Napa by ferry and electric train. When a pharmacy on Brown Street was available, she bought it in 1950. In 1952, she opened a second store at the Food City shopping center. There you could find the largest perfume department of any store in the area, with over two hundred different scents.

If your tastes ran to western clothing, you could stroll to the area now home to the Factory Outlets, which once held Purity Market, Allen and Benedict furniture store and the Saddle Shop, where all manner of tack and western clothing could be found. You could walk across the St. Helena Highway to shop because there was no freeway. All of North Napa was still ranches and open fields. That town of fewer than fourteen thousand souls—that "Pleasantville"—was to change dramatically in the coming decades. The essays in Part II paint pictures of life here from the 1950s to today.

When I moved to Napa, it seemed like a place that few strangers ever visited and few locals ever left, a kind of Brigadoon, where the narrow roads in and out of town were rarely traveled. Napa has been in a state of transformation

City of Napa garbage trucks, 1958. *Courtesy of Napa County Historical Society.*

ever since then, and my book seeks to document some of those changes. The final chapter is entitled "The Way We Live Today." It includes the new arrivals from as far as Vietnam, like Dr. Phong Vu, whose story is told in "A Fine State of Perfection." Immigrants like Jose Navarro journeyed from the state of Michoacan as Napa's wineries expanded; "Maria's Story" tells of his daughter's life. Families who have been in Napa for generations continue to honor their heritage, as do those described in "A Collins Family Christmas." This volume is a way of writing precious lives into history, those of the living and the dead, and making sure that their stories are not forgotten.

Chapter 6
The 1950s

"History Isn't Always Taught Properly": The Legacy of Ivy Loeber

The young Ivy Loeber "positively abhorred history." When Loeber entered the field of local history, it may have been with memories of her own youth and how disinterested she was in history—despite the fact that her own connection to Napa was so rich. Loeber's grandfather Calvin Griffith arrived in the Napa Valley in 1845, when it was still Mexican territory. Like most local men, he left town during the gold rush days and, as Miss Loeber put it, returned "when he realized he could get more 'gold' out of his farm than from the hills."

Ivy Loeber's father came to town from Baltimore. He wooed and wed her mother in Napa, where Ivy was born in 1880. Fifteen years later, Mr. Loeber moved his family back to Baltimore. Ivy told a reporter, "My father said he was raising three tomboys and he had to take them East so that they could become ladies." In the nineteenth century, "ladies" were distinguished from other women by their purity, piety and domesticity.

From the time she was sixteen, Ivy Loeber taught Sunday school, becoming the godmother of twenty-three children—"all ages, colors, and sexes." We don't have many details about Loeber's life in Baltimore before her return to Napa County. We do know that in the early twentieth century, spinsterhood was honored and allowed certain independence, so that Miss Loeber was able to devote herself to charity work outside the home. Once back in Napa,

Oak Knoll School, 1918. Ivy Loeber's sister is the teacher. Cathy Mathew's father, Cecil, is in the first seat on the far right, wearing overalls. *Courtesy of Cathy Mathews.*

she presided over the Women's Improvement Club and worked for the Red Cross. She also chaired the Well Baby Conference and helped distribute used clothing to poor mothers.

After World War II, Charles White of Calistoga "asked me to serve as chairman of a research committee in Napa County for the state centennial celebration in 1945." Thus, at the age of sixty-five, Ivy Loeber found a calling that would profoundly affect how Napans perceived and maintained their history. She helped organize the efforts by which St. Helena's Bale Mill became a state park. During a "Pioneer Picnic" held at the Old Bale Mill in May 1948, Loeber developed the vision of the Napa County Historical Society, which was incorporated by eighteen citizens a few days later at the Plaza Hotel on Brown Street in Napa. One of these was Ruth Bickford Northrup, who had lost her husband to pneumonia during World War II. Northrup would later serve as its president.

Ivy Loeber next set out on a lecture tour to speak about California history. She traveled to San Diego, Los Angeles, Fresno, Shasta and Sutter Counties. How illuminating it would be to read her letters or

Ruth Bickford married her high school sweetheart, Burr Northrup. She is pictured here with her husband and son in 1937. Eleven years later, she would be one of the founders of the Napa Country Historical Society. *Courtesy of Robert Northrup.*

diaries from this period, when few women were able to venture out of their own homes and towns!

We do have one letter that was written to her from Fred Levy. Levy wrote:

> *Harry Palmer, 85-years-old, a former stage driver in the valley, tells me that his grandfather and other pioneer men named the American Canyon for the few Americans living there. There were very few White settlers here in those days—they were mostly Indians and Mexicans, so they named the place where the White men resided, American Canyon.*

Ivy Loeber was both a historian of Napa and a teacher of Napa history. She told reporter Jerry Cornell, "As I see it, history isn't always taught properly in the classroom. There should be more emphasis on local history, on the romance of the past that's closest to home." In the 1950s, Napa's third graders studied Napa County history every year. Part of the experience was taking a trip on the school bus with Miss Loeber. Cathy Mathews remembers:

Miss Ivy M. Loeber giving a talk in the shadow of a mill wheel, Bale Mill, 1942–43. *Courtesy of Napa County Historical Society.*

In 1956, Mrs. Biava drove the Vichy school bus. We traveled to the Bale Mill, where we had a picnic. Then we went up on Glass Mountain to look for arrowheads. You could get really big pieces of obsidian. She would go out with us, and talk to us about what it was like for the Indians who lived in the area. She spoke about their extinction. She was tall and always wore dresses and high heels. Carefully dressed, her hair was always up in a French twist, her make-up and nails perfect...a very dignified looking woman. Even the rowdiest kids didn't mess around when she was there.

She really knew how to get kids' attention. She would go in the mill with us and talk about how the farmers brought in their wheat and corn to get it ground and what a major economic center the mill was for the valley. Back in the classroom, we had to do artwork about the trips we took. It would be presented at the Opera House at the end of the year. She would show up, and judge who got first, second, third prizes. Anybody who was in my classroom still remembers those trips with Ivy Loeber.

Loeber's influence and determination extended beyond the county line. The records of the Solano County Historical Society describe its founding "when an organizational meeting under the direction of Miss Ivy Loeber of St. Helena, was held at the old County Library in Fairfield." Ivy Loeber's articles can be found at the Napa Country Historical Society, but here is one of her stories:

Bale Mill, which became a state park in 1972. *Courtesy of Napa County Historical Society.*

May I tell you a story? A true story—the story of the beautiful Spanish mustard, a golden carpet of which now practically covers the floor of Napa Valley; but not only of Napa Valley—all of the valleys of California that were visited by the early Spanish Padres. This is the story of our early California when it was only a wilderness, with great quantities of trees, beautiful plants, all kinds of wild animals and birds; many, many Indians, and no white men at all. Father Serra had come from Spain to Mexico to spread the religion of Jesus Christ, and hearing about this beautiful, vast country to the north, decided to explore it. With a few faithful followers and Indian guides, he traveled north through what is now our glorious and loved California. As he traveled he scattered to the right, and to the left, the mustard seeds which he had brought with him from Spain.

The following year, as they returned south they followed "a ribbon of gold"; and following that path again Father Serra established his "Rosary of Missions," beginning in San Diego and ending in Sonoma. So wherever you see the Spanish mustard in California you know the Spanish fathers visited there. This is the early California legend as told to me by my Grandfather, whose father told it to him.

Napa's Unknown Brenda Starr

Brenda Starr, Reporter *was a comic strip about a glamorous, adventurous female reporter. It was created in 1940 by Dale Messick for the Chicago Tribune Syndicate. The character name was based on Brenda Frazier, a debutante of the 1930s, while her appearance was based on the movie actress Rita Hayworth. The strip initially encountered resistance from* Tribune *editor Joseph Patterson because its creator was a woman.*

While today women make important contributions to newspapers and local magazines, newspaperwomen in the 1940s and '50s like Phyllis King were unusual. Phyllis King was one of the few pioneer journalists who kept her job after World War II. King's daughter, Liz Reyna, writes of her mother:

Phyllis King Thompson was a newspaper reporter during the 1940s through the early Sixties, mostly in Napa, her birthplace. Her great-grandfather, a Methodist minister, had come here in the 1880s after serving as a chaplain for the Union Army in the Civil War, and as a circuit riding minister in

California's mining towns. Her grandfather, Judge Percy King, presided over Napa courts from Prohibition through World War II. Her father Percy King Jr. was also a judge in the 1950s and her Aunt "Babe" (Elizabeth King Robinson) was Napa's first woman lawyer.

Phyllis, born in 1924, graduated from Napa High in 1942, attended Stanford and then moved to Marysville and worked on a daily paper during World War II. The public relations officer at nearby Camp Beale was Carl F. Beuoy, whom she would contact for camp news and later married. After the war ended, the couple moved to the Midwest, where they both sought work in journalism. Their two children were born in 1947 and 1948, but their marriage didn't last. Daughter Liz explains:

After my mother separated from my dad, she moved back to Napa. We lived at the ranch at 2230 Big Ranch Road for a while, then moved to downtown Napa where we lived in an old Victorian on Second Street. This is where most of my mom's newspaper career took place. She was a versatile

Phyllis King with her son Phillip and daughter Liz, 1949. *Courtesy of Liz Reyna.*

reporter, covering everything from what was then called "women's news" to politics, major news stories, travel, and scientific advances. She had a terrific sense of humor, a very quick mind, knew everyone in town, and was a very social person. She had reddish brown hair, gorgeous and naturally wavy, was always slim and enjoyed up-to-date styles.

Reyna describes how her mother simultaneously worked in a "man's world," as it was then frankly labeled, and also managed to "wallpaper several tall rooms in her old Victorian with only the help of two young children." Reyna remembers watching her mother sitting at her typewriter, either at home or at the *Napa Register* office, with the phone cradled on her shoulder, getting information on some breaking news and pounding away at her keyboard at the same time:

Within moments the story would roll out of the typewriter, a finished product requiring only minor edits before it would appear in the next day's paper. She worked a full day at the Register, *and then came home to write Napa stories for the* Sacramento Bee *and the* Oakland Tribune. *By*

Napa Register Building, 1906, where Phyllis King worked. *Courtesy of Napa County Historical Society.*

Phyllis King with her colleagues at the *Napa Register*. *Courtesy of Liz Reyna.*

> *9 p.m., we would drive down to the bus depot to send the stories off for the morning's editions.*

Phyllis King herself gives a vivid account of what it was like to work for a local paper in the '40s. She describes working with *Register* editor Arthur MacKay "in the days when reporters used folded over half sheets of copy paper to be held easily in the left hand...before they donned horned rimmed glasses and bought clipboards."

> *Mac's predecessor was a fellow by the name of George Peck...When George arrived in Napa, about 1941, the newsroom stretched some 15 by 12 feet, room enough for him, a reporter, and the society editor plus the morgue. The society editor had a constant flow of people in to inform her of "club happenings."*
>
> *Back in those days, people in town hung out at the Plaza Hotel bar. George used to get together there every night with the lawyers, courthouse*

personnel, and other interested townsfolk. One night he became deeply engrossed in conversation with a group…until he decided maybe he couldn't make it to his rooming house three blocks away. He went to the phones and called an ambulance!

King recounts how newspapers were produced during the war years: "In order to catch the mail, the paper had to turn from an evening to a morning publication, so the society editor handled things during the day, with the reporter and editor coming in late in the afternoon." The publisher and composing room foreman got the paper out in the morning. Liz Reyna concludes:

Mom died too early, at 49, more than 30 years ago. Her stories offered glimpses into other simpler times: when Napa's population was only 13,000, before Berryessa Valley was flooded, when a new house was $11,000, and the Uptown Theatre was showing Teenage Rebel. *As the years pass, her old stories from high school and her many newspaper clippings, are becoming brittle and yellowed with age…like a bottle cast on the shore, they bring us back something of the person Mom was.*

Phyllis King's writing transports us to old Napa, where people gathered downtown at the Plaza Hotel Bar, a time when everyone read the daily newspaper, which held those thirteen thousand souls together in community—the world that she chronicled with such delight.

What West Park Was

Local history satisfies an innate human desire to be connected to a place. It feeds our hunger to experience life directly and on intimate terms. It serves nostalgia, which is arguably as compelling a cultural force as the quest for progress.
—Joseph Amato, Rethinking Home

As Paula Amen Judah and I researched material for our book *Napa Valley Farming*, we were graced with the reminiscences of Carolyn Salazar, whose great-grandfather Johan Knief left Germany to settle and farm in Browns Valley in 1854 with his family. When Johan's son Louis married Caroline Wohrman, both families continued to farm in Browns Valley, while Caroline Wohrman's parents raised fruits and vegetables for the thriving Soda Springs Resort off Soda Canyon Road.

Louis and Caroline Knief's son, Ernest F. Knief Sr., was born in Napa in 1894. In 1911, at the age of seventeen, he began working at Mare Island Naval Shipyard, from which he retired in 1957 as a leading man in Shop #31. His daughter Carolyn writes, "However, he loved farming, and prior to his marriage to Lillian Ransford in 1934, he purchased 20 acres of land in Napa off of West Park Avenue." Ten acres extended from West Park Avenue over to Pueblo Avenue, just north of where the West Park School now lies. Their land was on both sides of West Park Avenue.

The family built their home and barn nearest to the creek. The Kniefs had fruit trees, a berry patch and vegetable gardens. Ernest Jr. was a member of Future Farmers of America (FFA) when he was in high school. Through FFA, he raised steers, which he sold at the county fair, and turkeys, which he sold just before Thanksgiving. Carolyn remembers:

> *We always had dogs and cats, and one year my sister, Beth, my brother, Ernie Jr., and I traded some ducks for a goose from a neighbor boy. Happy, our*

Ernest F. Knief Sr. and his daughters, Bethel and Carolyn, in front of their cherry orchard, 1942. *Courtesy of Carolyn Salazar.*

> *goose, lived for many years and was a wonderful pet. Several years we also boarded a horse that belonged to our dad's friend, George Vienop. Other pets over the years included rabbits, squirrels, hamsters, ducks and chickens. I have fond memories of picking berries with Mom, Beth and Ernie Jr., and all of us slicing peaches, arranging them on trays to be dried in a covering Pop had prepared. I also enjoyed helping shuck the field corn after it had dried. The corn and wheat were mostly used for our own farm livestock and poultry.*

Originally, the Kniefs' orchard was half prune and half cherry trees. In the late 1940s, the cherry trees became diseased, and they had to be torn out. Mr. Knief replanted the land in corn and wheat over the following years, along with a small orchard of Alberta peaches. Carolyn writes:

> *Although still quite young at the time that my dad removed the cherry trees, I remember when all the stumps were burned, and neighbors gathered round to watch the flames. The glow lit up the night sky. After Pop planted the wheat fields, and the grain was harvested, one year the shaft was put into bales. We had fun making forts out of the bales until they were sold. I always enjoyed riding on his caterpillar tractor with him, or riding on the drag (which leveled off the plowed ground) when he plowed our fields. At times Pop would find a baby Jackrabbit in the fields when he was plowing. He would bring it in to us and we would raise it.*

Mr. Knief hired crews each summer to help pick the prunes. He grew three types: French (a rather small prune); Imperial, which were large and meaty; and Sugar, which were mid-sized. In the evenings, after he got home from work at Mare Island, and during his summer vacation times, he, along with family and some crew, stacked the boxes of prunes on a flatbed truck and took them to the barn area to be dipped in a lye solution and set out to dry on trays in the sun. Prunes that did not contain enough sugar would turn brown and shrivel. These brown prunes, called "chocolates," were picked from the trays and discarded. The good prunes were sold to the Sunsweet facilities in Napa. In addition to the prunes, the family also picked and sliced the peaches. These were dried in a sulfa smoke and also sold to Sunsweet. Carolyn recalls:

> *I enjoyed spraying the prune trees to protect them from various diseases. Pop would fill the stray rig with water and the chemicals needed for the spray. We*

Carolyn Knief at bat, about 1953. Behind her are the windmill, the cornfield and the eastern hills. *Courtesy of Carolyn Salazar.*

> *would dress up in oversized rain slickers and hats, put some type of mask over our noses and mouths so that we would not breathe in the chemicals, and climb up onto the top of the spray rig. Pop would drive his tractor, pulling the spray rig, up and down the rows of prune trees while we, holding nozzled hoses, would spray the trees. I also loved riding on the flatbed truck and helping gather the boxes of prunes, the evenings of dipping the prunes. I remember the nights when we would have a summer rainstorm, and all the family would rush out to the fields to stack the trays of prunes so that they wouldn't get wet.*

As Napa began to grow, it became more difficult to move the farm equipment across West Park Avenue to plow under the prune trees, so Mr. Knief sold the ten acres to the north of West Park Avenue in the late 1940s or early 1950s. He continued farming the other ten acres until about 1965, when he sold most of his land. The Creekside Glen housing development stands there now. Ernest Knief passed away in 1969, and Carolyn's mother, Lillian, followed in 1993. The family home, now on Bradford Street, still remains in the Knief family. Carolyn concludes:

> *Farming is not easy, and my dad's work at Mare Island helped to fully support his family, but I would not exchange the wonderful experiences of my childhood on our farm in Napa for anything. The working together as a family, the enjoying the fresh fruits and vegetables grown, are things that many people cannot experience today.*

Every December, Mr. Knief would place Christmas lights in two of the tall fir trees by their home, and they could be seen all the way down West Park Avenue. I like to think that the remembered glow of those lights still shines on the people of the West Park neighborhood.

Chapter 7
The 1960s

Searching for Peggy Connolly

The Connolly Ranch is quietly and effectively offering us a rare sensory impression of rural life in a rapidly subdividing Napa. The lowing of its cows, the murmuring of its chickens, the bleating of its baby goats conjure sights, sounds and smells of a bygone era. I've been curious for years about how the ranch was saved as a public resource by its last occupant, Peggy Connolly. Harold Kelly, community activist, tells the story:

> *Her family owned the ranch. I knew Helen, the older sister, and Peggy, the last remaining sister. They visited the ranch regularly as children and young adults; it was their summer place. Sometime in the '60s, the sisters moved full time to the ranch. I was active in the Browns Valley Area, and Helen got involved with the neighborhood association. Her sister Peggy was supportive of things we were working on…they were among the original signers of Measure J. When I got to know Peggy Connolly, I enjoyed listening to her as she spoke of how much pleasure she got from watching children feed her animals. She told me she would like to see children continue to learn about farm life and so left her property to The Land Trust telling me, "Do what is right." She died a few months later.*

I found an article by Kevin Courtney about Connolly Ranch, written in 2004. He quotes Marilyn Warnock, family friend. When I located Marilyn in Rio Vista, she told me that her mother and aunt had attended the University of California–Berkeley with Peggy Connolly. Peggy and her sister Helen had grown up in San

Connolly sister at the ranch. *Courtesy of Connolly Ranch.*

Francisco, where their father was a pharmacist. As adults, the Connelly sisters lived in a Telegraph Hill apartment, where Peggy worked as a juvenile probation officer and Helen as a court reporter.

Marilyn Warnock's parents moved to the Veterans' Home in Yountville, and the Connolly sisters retired to live full time at the ranch in Napa. Marilyn's family frequently visited the Connolly sisters' ranch, where she kept Marilyn's horse, Cookie. Warnock also remembers "a sweet little dog named Miss Mitzie, who ruled the roost... the fantastic library and wonderful old furniture and lots of potlucks, sitting under the oak tree."

Marilyn's sister, Lorie Saxon, told me that often she would take a semester off of college to spend time on the ranch:

> *Peggy and Helen were very special and unusual people; you knew that if you knew them for more than five minutes. I remember them as being unusually intelligent women, something I was always looking for. Always a step or two ahead. Peggy looked like an Irish Coleen, with a lovely smile.*

I asked Lorie to describe a typical day at the ranch:

> *I always thought of it as the Chisholm Trail, going up to the house. They wore pants and sweaters and housedresses; if it was a hot day, they offered iced tea or iced coffee, then they broke out the highballs on*

the porch. They had donkeys and cats. They were very, very opinionated and had wonderful senses of humor. They would be so happy to know that someone appreciated them.

Marilyn's brother, Roger Andrews, wrote:

Peggy and Helen, our "bogus aunts" as they often called themselves, probably left many friends and admirers but likely no real enemies, and precious few of any of them are still alive. Peggy and Helen were in some ways larger than life figures. They were smart—maybe brilliant. They were plain-spoken, no nonsense women who could—and did—take on anyone who crossed them. With their brother and father, and those who worked for them occasionally at the ranch, I recall them as caring and compassionate. With just about everyone else (us included), they were a bit rough and tumble, none too careful about their language, yet always ready for a good laugh, and always good hearted with a strong sense of fairness.

Peggy Connolly died in 1991, and the beloved oak tree was struck by lightning in the late '90s. I used to walk my dog outside the ranch, listening at

A child at Connolly Ranch. *Courtesy of Oscar Vega.*

dusk for the sounds of the geese and the chickens, imagining this land back before the traffic. Lately, I've been watching my grandson and hundreds of other children excitedly jostle to feed the sheep and the goats. Peggy and Helen's ranch is a living legacy, an act of great love for the children of the future in a world the Connolly sisters would not live to see.

REMEMBERING NAPA'S SERVICE STATIONS

And there's where (during the day) mom would stop for gas,
a Shell filling station in the curve at the foot of a long hill,
a couple of pumps and a little office and a double bay
over which "Service is our Business" shone in red plastic

as the smiling proprietor emerged, wiping his large hands,
looking like Glenn Miller on the 78 rpm records she'd play
(I still have them, maiden initials scratched on each label),
Like some veteran still wearing his crisp khaki uniform.
—Michael McFee, "Service Is Our Business"

Downtown Napa in the 1960s. *Courtesy of Mr. M.*

After World War II, affordable cars and access to cheap gasoline created an economy in which most families were able to buy a car. Former Napan Paula Amen Judah recalls:

> *When I was a kid, a man named Max had a gas station by Silverado Meat Market. He would hurry over to our Kaiser, stuffing his grease rag in his back pocket, then lean towards the window as my mother rolled it down, and say, "Fill it up?" I had my first Coca-Cola at a gas station, in a short green bottle, with a metal cap—the opener was right there on the machine. I remember a garage on the right and a little office on the left, with huge glass windows, the pin-up calendar on the wall inside. The men were calm, competent and strong, and they knew all about cars.*

Cathy Mathews describes John Grippi's Flying A station, also on Silverado Trail, where other East Napans stopped.

> *My grandmother loved him…John would look under the hood and say, "Mrs Russell, there's a little something wrong. You need to take it to Vito Grossi's* [next to the fairgrounds]. *" You got your windshield done every time, and he always checked your wipers and your oil.*

Pete Gasser's Dodge and Plymouth dealership featured a lubritorium. *Courtesy of Napa County Historical Society.*

Mathews also remembers Primo Colla's Shell station on Lincoln and Silverado—"an incredibly good looking guy, one of the first people in town to have a car wash." *Register* writer Pat Stanley noted the change of ownership of Colla's Shell at Lincoln Avenue and Silverado Trail. It was sold by proprietor Larry Hansen after twenty-eight years. Stanley writes:

> *Hansen has been a familiar figure in front of the station, waving to friends and customers, smoking a pipe or walking his 7-year-old Jack Russell terrier, Billie, when not pumping gas. This year, 45 days of rain within two months kept customers away from the car wash he installed 18 years ago: "Not many people pay for a car wash when God will wash it for free," he said.*

Gas was fifty-seven cents a gallon when Hansen opened the doors in February 1978, purchasing the stations from the handsome Primo Colla. Patrick Scott was hired while still in high school and eventually became station manager; at one time or another, Scott's four brothers also worked at Colla's Shell. As many as five different families have been supported by the station. Pat Stanley notes:

> *Hansen, 60, said he's too young to retire. "I cannot not work," he said. "I'll get a job. I can't stop working. I'll really miss seeing my friends and customers," he said. "That's what I enjoyed the most. I'll dearly miss them and want to thank Napa."*

Joe Cetwinski sold his Joe's Chevron station on Trancas Street in 2006, also after twenty-eight years. Cathy Mathews remembers how Cetwinski always sponsored crab feeds to benefit countless local charities. Jerry Davis adds regretfully, "I used to get lunch at that station…the owner was given thirty days to get out."

Each of us longtime Napans has a full-service gas station in our pasts. I remember Napa's independently owned and operated service stations, where men like Roy Bennett on Third Street and Milt Totman on Solano greeted customers. As a young mother, I took this help for granted; it had been there all my life. Although we joke that the past always *seems* better, in terms of service to drivers, the "old days" *were* better. The automobile industry created service stations in the 1920s in order to help Americans handle the enormous responsibilities of maintaining an automobile. We

Betty Hopperstad with her beloved VW bus and son David Kramer, 1982. *Courtesy of Betty Hopperstad.*

felt cared for, secure and safe. One of these stations was operated by my children's grandfather, John McCune, in Oakville. Michael McFee's poem concludes:

> *That station's long gone. Now it's ten pumps and a mini-mart.*
> *Service was his business. And service was her business, too,*
> *a mother serving children every day for over twenty years*
> *until they were old enough to drive their cars away from her.*

FANCY FAIRE AND COMMUNITY PROJECTS

Commonly, scholars of history recognize a few women who were famous nationally for their public contributions. But we cannot leave history to the scholars alone. Women's history must encompass not only the stories of renowned national figures but also the quiet heroism of ordinary citizens. Every town has a responsibility to note and remember its own.

Napa Baths was an indoor pool and steam room located at the present site of Community Projects thrift shop. *Courtesy of Mr. M.*

A traditional way women contribute to their towns is through charity work. One example would be craft fairs organized throughout the community, such as the popular "fancy fairs" Community Projects, Inc. (CP), held at the fairgrounds for many years. We know that Fancy Faire was created by the women of CP, but what is the organization's history? Where did the organization begin? How did it run so successfully, and who were the personalities that kept Community Projects thriving since its inception in 1918? By talking to just one person, the origin of this important history begins to unspool.

MaryEllen Simmons was one of hundreds of women who belonged to Community Projects. Her memories, as a newcomer and, later, as its 1975–76 board president, begin to paint a picture of the organization. She remembers becoming aware of Community Projects "by following CP in the newspaper. I was impressed by what the organization did…great things were accomplished as a group that one could never accomplish alone."

MaryEllen reminiscences, "I was working as a checker at Food Fair Market on Silverado Trail in 1963 when Pat (Vernice) Gasser approached me about joining. Pat emphasized the organization was one of work, with camaraderie, yes, but with all things done through work, not pure socialization." Gasser's mother had been a founder of the group, whose first project was rolling bandages for soldiers wounded in World War I.

Vernice (Pat) Stoddard Gasser, one of the founders of Community Projects, Inc. *Courtesy of the Peter and Vernice Gasser Foundation.*

The overall mission of Community Projects, MaryEllen recalls, was "to benefit the people of Napa County." Members were required to log a minimum number of volunteer hours and attend monthly meetings, which MaryEllen describes as "all business" with an agenda that included a strict accounting by the board of directors for every penny brought in and spent. During her time there, CP purchased a new van for Napa Valley Head Start, replaced Red Cross vehicles and gave countless scholarships to local high school students. She remembers learning that an early project had been to raise enough money to purchase a whole set of dishes for the Parks Victory Hospital, which once stood on a tree-lined Jefferson Street.

Years later, Community Projects became the auxiliary support for the new hospital, Queen of the Valley, founded in 1958, where CP greeters in their blue monogrammed smocks were a welcome sight to patients and visitors. That affiliation generated the organization's principle that "no CP volunteer would ever fill a job that should be done by a trained, paid employee." Many of the women fulfilled their hours by working at the Thrift Shop on Franklin Street. MaryEllen describes a typical day at the Thrift Shop:

> *Volunteers arrived, bag lunch in hand, and gathered in the back room where donations were stored. They unpacked, sorted, mended, and priced items. In the early years of the store, if clothing arrived soiled or wrinkled, the women themselves would take it home to launder, iron, and return.*

The shop's annual Spring Opening became a much-anticipated event in the community, and the Thrift Store expanded, buying the service station next door when it closed down. Community Projects also took on the project of coordinating all the transportation for the Kaiser Golf Tournament (later

Opening of the Kaiser International Golf Tournament, circa 1970. Dr. B. Butler, George Simmons, Maryellen Simmons, Orva Honadel, Jane Butler, Jean Jaimson and Jane Morrell. *Courtesy of Paula Amen Schmitt.*

Anheiser-Busch). The tournament became one of the organization's major fundraisers, but CP's annual Fancy Faire remained its signature event for many years.

Preparation and planning for Fancy Faire was an enormous undertaking. The women worked in their homes year-round making craft items and preparing baked goods and other consumables. They and their entire families invested hours of sweat labor, transforming a cold exhibition building into a festive and beautiful place to kick off Napa's holiday season.

Fancy Faire is gone, but Community Projects thrives, with new generations of women joining the organization. Women's history—the stories that women tell—can restore to us the memory of Fancy Faire, the triumph of Community Projects, ventures that knitted our community together in charity and craft.

Chapter 8
The 1970s

Feminism Finds Napa

When I went to college there was no women's history. Well, that is inaccurate. There has always been women's history; it is just that, until the late sixties, no one was looking for it, looking at it, or teaching it.
—*Carol Kammen,* On Doing Local History

For Napa, as well as the rest of the country, the 1970s were a time of political awakenings and activism. In those days, social problems seemed imminently fixable, and women across the country set about to challenge the status quo. In 1972, a group of young Napa women rented a downtown storefront at 1783 Third Street. They named it the Napa Women's Center and scheduled events on a nightly basis.

One of the members of the Women's Center, teacher Lois Engle, developed a slide show about sexism in children's nursery rhymes. The ideas and spirit of the Women's Center weren't confined within its walls, as Engle wrote an article about feminism and child rearing for the Kiwanis Club's Ladies' Night. Jay Goetting and Jane Myers invited women to speak about feminism to a radio program on KVON.

Members of the center, like Kit Hall, Judy Nelson and Jan Svoboda, campaigned for a women's reentry program and a child-care center at Napa College because the feminist movement was encouraging so many to return to school. Carol Raahauge Grant became one of the first

"Women Who Made History in Napa" were honored at Napa College in 1983: Hope Lugo, Serena Cochran, Elsie Crane and Maryellen Boyet. *Courtesy of Lauren Coodley.*

women's studies teachers at Napa College, with now-forgotten courses on marriage and the family. Serena Cochran created a class on single parenting. One of the most popular courses, taught by Evie Trevethan, was assertiveness training. A group of young students and teachers that included Ann Schwartz, Linda Schoppert, Dana Hiney, Betty Hopperstad and Lauren Coodley initiated a volunteer hotline for battered women, the first of its kind in Napa. Others created a slideshow on the links between pornography and violence against women.

Across town, June Stephenson had applied for a job as principal at Redwood Junior High School. She remembers the president of the school board saying to her that since he "thought I looked pretty, how would I be able to tell men what to do?" The school settled out of court for the difference between what she would have been paid as a principal and what she made as a dean. Stephenson found a copy of *A Short History of Women*, published in 1928, and she recalls:

> *I hadn't known there was a women's history. The Social Studies Department at Napa High didn't want a course in women's history, but Tom Fotinos agreed...he saved the course. Students said they had learned more about history than any history course they'd taken.*

Michele Jones became a machinist in the 1970s. *Courtesy of Michele Jones Smith.*

Stephenson left teaching to write her own book, *Women's Roots*. After her departure, women's history was again removed from the curriculum at Napa High and was only offered at Hill and Valley, a school program for pregnant teenagers created and taught by Sudie Pollack. Pollack also developed Women's History Week celebrations in the public schools, which were held throughout the 1980s, while there was an active feminist movement in Napa.

Mary Ellen Boyet was one of the organizers of a vibrant chapter of the National Women's Political Caucus, which helped elect women to local and state office. Dorothy Searcy became one of the first women on the city council, and Ginny Sims was the first woman on the board of supervisors. By 1981, a petition campaign to the board of supervisors—and years of collecting signatures at shopping centers—resulted in the opening of a shelter for battered women and their children.

One of the key tenets of feminism was that women should be economically self-sufficient. Apprenticeships in blue-collar jobs offered new opportunities, and many Napa women applied for and received that training. One of them was Michelle Jones, who was hired as a machinist's helper at Kaiser in 1978.

Within three days, she was promoted to apprentice—the first time ever for a woman. Michelle remembers the encouragement she received from machine shop instructor Arendt Wheeler at Napa College. Interviewed in 1980, she told *Register* reporter Laura Thomas, "I feel secure and good that I have a trade now."

At the same time as affirmative action was helping women into the trades across the country, threats to unionized workers increased when President Reagan fired all air traffic controllers, including one woman who worked at the Napa Airport. Many supporters of women's equality recognized the need to support women's rights and highlight the struggles of female workers. In Napa, clerks at Carithers, the last union department store in Napa, went on strike when they were asked to take a pay cut in 1981. At that time, I described some of them:

> *Loretta wears her dark hair upswept into a bun, is proud of her knowledge of jewelry and her "smart mouth," lives in a trailer with her pigtailed daughter, has diabetes. Marlene is a warm rosy woman at midlife. With essential dignity and self-respect, she picketed in her bathing suit, brought iced tea and a beach umbrella to the line.*

The Women's Political Caucus collected canned food for the strikers and organized benefits, including movie nights and dances at the Labor Temple on Main Street. Inspired by films documenting women's early labor struggles, the youngest striker, nineteen, brought her infant to the picket line in a stroller adorned with a sign reading "Don't Be a Scab." Linda Dietiker-Yolo, member of the Napa County Commission on the Status of Women, wrote to the manager of Carithers: "If the shocking plight of these women is not entirely as represented, perhaps you will inform us. Otherwise, we ask that justice be instituted at Carithers."

The women won their strike, and they credited the community for its support. Carithers striker Bonnie Lee Barnhill described their victory as "one giant step for womankind." Their newsletter noted:

> *It was like David slaying Goliath: a relative handful of determined union women picketed their employer, Carithers, part of a mammoth corporation—in order to maintain a decent living standard and win dignity in their place of work. They never gave up. They walked for four and one half months, from the beginning of spring on through the parching heat of summer.*

Carithers workers win their strike, 1981. *Courtesy of Lauren Coodley.*

When the manufacturing of clothing was moved out of America, the unionized jobs in those factories disappeared. As clothes became cheaper and cheaper, wages and conditions in retail stores plummeted in Napa, as well as across the nation. Maria Brambila writes, "I began working at the garment factory Rough Rider, and then it was bought out by the Koret Company. I worked at this company for almost 10 years, until the Koret Company went out of business." One by one, factories in Napa closed—Rough Rider shut its doors in 1976 and Kaiser Steel in 1983.

Michele Jones was injured at work and was never able to return to her job as a machinist. However, the movement she had been a part of survived, though mostly misunderstood or unrecorded by history. The women's movement of the 1970s was not about helping a few women climb the corporate ladder. Instead, it was about women standing together to protect one another, to expand opportunities and to fight for fairness for all. This movement allowed me to be employed as the only full-time female professor of history to ever teach at Napa Valley College.

MRS. BREWSTER'S DOUBLE LIFE

In 1960, Rachel Friedman moved here with her husband, Larry, and two young children. They partnered with her brother, Harris Nussbaum, and her father, Morris, to run Brewsters. Back then, Napa had a population of about fifteen thousand people. Rachel remembers, "When I first moved to Napa, my comment was 'I feel like I'm moving to the end of the world.'" Back then,

Rachel Friedman as a young mother with Sandy and Laurie. *Courtesy of Rachel Friedman.*

Trancas was the north edge of town, uncrowded and barely developed with only the newly built hospital and some Italian and Chinese restaurants, reminiscent of Napa's early immigrants. The Friedmans bought a home in the just-built Bel Aire subdivision. Rachel remembers, "Bel Aire Plaza housed only Montgomery Ward, the bowling alley and Levinson's Drugs, which had moved out there." But she also recalls "no competition for shopping—everyone went downtown."

She describes Napa in those days as a "real country town where everyone was very friendly." Brewsters supplied work clothes, boots, bedding, cots and almost anything else that the vineyard workers needed to survive; when the store had an outdoor sale, shoppers lined up for blocks. Louis Martini would drive up in his Cadillac clad in overalls. The Brewsters ads were a highlight of the *Napa Register*, with their zany caricatures of Rachel, Larry and the crew. But this is the story of what the *Register*, in 1986, called Rachel's "double life"—the career she created beyond the women's department of Brewsters, with its "reasonably priced, timely fashions for women of all ages and sizes."

Rachel had earned her undergraduate degree in child development around 1950, "but there were very few jobs to go with that degree." Rachel had moved to Napa as a mother of two children; she gave birth to two more children and enrolled them in what was one of the first preschools in Napa, operated by Jen Terrace. Rachel worked in the classroom in trade for her kids' tuition and describes Jen Terrace with admiration as "the mother of early childhood development in Napa."

It was through Jen, who worked at Head Start, that Rachel became interested in that program, then still part of the school district. She was inspired by its successful outreach to families and eagerly joined the Head Start advisory board. She began teaching at Head Start and enrolled in Sonoma State University for her teaching credential, earning a master's degree in early childhood education at the age of fifty.

Ad for Brewster's marking the wedding anniversary of the Friedmans. *Courtesy of Rachel Friedman.*

In the '70s, the County Office of Education was located next door to Brewsters when the federal government passed a law requiring counties to offer education to special needs preschoolers for the first time. Rachel recounts:

> *The superintendent was a buddy of Larry. He called me up one day and said, "We're starting this program, I spoke to Larry and he said it was okay for me to hire you. I was so incensed that he would ask Larry before he would ask me!*

Rachel accepted the position, and in the preschool program she designed, "you could meet families and become close to your students, because you cannot change a child's life without having some contact with families." From that first moment in 1976, Rachel was a working teacher, still full of energy when she finally retired in 2000 at the age of seventy. "And believe me I saw miracles, I saw miracles happen…I saw children blossom, kids that had been given up on—that was the fuel for me." Tammy Rogers, Rachel's classroom aide, says:

> *What really amazed me was working with her in the classroom; she would hold two kids on each leg and still be able to talk to the moms and do paperwork. If it hadn't been for Rachel, I would have never have gone back to school to become a teacher…I would never have known about potato pancakes…she celebrated Hanukah along with Christmas and Kwanza with the toddlers.*

At the community college where Carol Kelly hired Rachel to teach in the Early Childhood Education program, she created a new class aimed at educating preschool teachers about special needs children. In 1983, Rachel and her brother, Harris Nussbaum, were both honored as Teacher of the Year in Napa. Rachel comments that she was called "Mr. Nussbaum's sister" when she visited his class as a guest speaker and "Mr. Brewster's wife" in the store.

In the '70s, while some Napans favored what looked like a revitalization of downtown, many businesspeople questioned the benefits of redevelopment. A group of Main Street merchants formed Citizens Against the Destruction of Napa, using Brewsters as a meeting place. Friedman's husband, Larry, particularly opposed the construction of a clock tower on First Street and took his fight all the way to the California Supreme Court, where the case was lost.

In 1986, the most devastating flood in one hundred years hit the town, as the Napa River rose to levels none living had seen before. Nearly five thousand people were evacuated, 250 homes were destroyed and three people died. Soscol Avenue turned into a river, most of Napa's businesses were damaged from the floodwaters and the downtown stores were drenched with mud. According to the *Register*, "Larry Friedman thanked his employees for saving the rest of the store by stacking sandbags until almost midnight; nobody has flood insurance. 'If there's such a thing as an off the floor sale we'll have one,' Friedman joked."

But the drought years that followed eliminated Brewsters' wet gear business. Two years after the flood, the town council voted to approve a Target Store in the Bel Aire shopping center, and Brewsters lost much of its camping gear sales. In 1998, when no buyer for the store could be found, Larry and Rachel decided it was time to close. Kevin Courtney reported:

Rachel and Larry going to the Chamber of Commerce dinner in December 1974. *Courtesy of Rachel Friedman.*

News of Brewsters demise had shaken a lot of old-time customers. "I had a woman break into tears. She said, 'What am I going to do? I've been coming here as a child.' When Larry made an appearance at the store Tuesday, a shopper came up to the busy shopkeeper and whispered, 'This is history.'"

Larry Friedman died in 2005. At his funeral, the mayor sat shoulder to shoulder with store employees like Don Stern and Artie Kinney. Vineyard workers paid their respects alongside parents and children taught by Rachel. There was an entire row of homeless people whom Larry had befriended. Tammy Rogers remembers that "it was the very first time I'd ever gone to a Jewish synagogue. It was beautiful…all kinds of people, all cultures and backgrounds. As I sat there, I looked around and thought—what a life."

Rachel Nussbaum Friedman celebrated her eightieth birthday in downtown Napa at Buckhorn's Restaurant. Today, Rachel's legacy runs like a river through all the children and mothers whose lives she touched—what a life, indeed!

Since her eightieth birthday, Rachel has learned to play African drums and is currently in a ukulele club. She paints with watercolors once a month with a group of friends and serves food at the Neighborhood Table to Napa's homeless once a month. She writes, "I am still on the substitute list and keep my involvement with teaching and working with young children with special needs. I wish I were young again and could get back in the world of early childhood intervention."

TREASURES OF TERRACE DRIVE

Ten Kinds of Snakes

Is what he remembers: finding them in
those open fields between farmhouses,
meadows where poor kids like him
could feast on nature.
—Lauren Coodley

Sometimes history offers itself in a casual conversation; sometimes it arrives in the form of a letter in the mail. Linda McElroy wrote to me in 2008:

> *I have thought many times to contact you to see if you might wish to explore a piece of Napa Paradise before it is transformed. My grandparents, John and Theresa Maddalena, purchased a three acre farm for $8,000, in 1943…a two bedroom house, two car garage, four small rentals, one and a half acre pasture for the milk cow, chicken*

> *house, rabbit house, feed and shop rooms. Built in 1935 mostly of redwood, the buildings are in decay. The property is at 1111 Terrace Drive, about two blocks from the Tulocay Cemetery.*
>
> *My family is now pushing to bulldoze and sell to a developer...I am on a familial archaeological dig, becoming more involved each day...I have great rabbit coop doors, farm implements, and I have not explored the garage loft yet. Most recent treasures: my grandfather's copper still, which he used for making grappa, a stationary box with letters from Italy written 1910–1922.*

Librarian Stephanie Grohs and I stepped onto Linda's porch on a cold winter afternoon. We immediately felt the poignancy of this farm, with its haunting reminder of the unvarnished nature of rural life in Napa throughout most of the last century. We often forget that land was inexpensive here until the 1990s. Even people of modest means could own a home in the country and raise their children there.

Farm at Terrace Drive, bunkhouse. *Courtesy of Carolyn Younger.*

Typically, the homes of the less prosperous are not among those preserved; thus, our images and impressions of the past are incomplete. The plain farmhouses, the rusting equipment, the quiet meadows are too often destroyed. Beautiful downtown Victorians are not the only homes Napans once inhabited, yet they often define Napa's history. There on Terrace Drive lies another truth. Historian Joseph Amato explains:

> *Before there were trucks and stereo systems, tract houses and motorcycles, the air was filled with other sounds. It was the roar of nature that set the evening ambience: a hubbub generated by millions of water fowl, amphibians, beetles, bugs, and birds, grasshoppers and a myriad of other creatures that thrived in the small lakes and ponds and wetlands.*

Although the Maddalena farm has been sold, before Linda McElroy passed the keys to the new owner, she generously made the farm available to students working on the Napa Grid Project. Carolyn Younger has shared the photographs she took from that period for this book.

Many Napans have fond memories of the baseball diamond at the top of "the field," the enormous open area between Hoffman Avenue and the two ends of Terrace Drive. Paula Amen Judah writes:

> *I remember going up to the diamond for a big gathering of little girls interested in playing softball—my sister Shirley and I walked up from home with our baseball gloves and our own bat. I remember being put on the Orioles team—they gave us all purple T-shirts with the team name on it. I wonder if others remember that ball diamond, the air raid station—a little building where volunteers watched the skies for unknown aircraft during World War Two—or the playground with swings & merry-go-round. I wonder who else remembers playing there, running through the weeds, picking cattails in the swamp.*

From Jeff Green, I learned how this park was saved:

> I was a reporter with the Napa County Record *from 1973 to 1976. I was covering the Napa City Council, and at one meeting a citizen came to the council with a proposal to build tennis courts on surplus land. The city administrators looked around and decided that nobody was using Fairview Park.*

Farm at Terrace Drive, workshop. *Courtesy of Carolyn Younger.*

Green suspected otherwise and checked with a friend who grew up near the park. He learned that kids still went there to play ball, so:

> *I decided I'd go bang on some doors in the neighborhood…I went up and down a couple streets and everyone was 100 percent opposed…They*

mounted a big drive to save the park, and marched on city hall. The city backed off.

Fairview Park was preserved. Shortly afterward, in 1978, Nancy Manahan moved to Terrace Drive. She writes:

What I remember is the sensation of suddenly being in the country...a large pasture edged with lemon, fig, prune, plum, and apricot trees. My partner Barbara Evans and I lived in one of the six cottages at 1066, and my sister Margaret lived next door. Up the hill sat Dewey Anderson's home and the garage that had housed his automotive repair business. Dewey, a wonderful landlord, kept the property in good repair and spent time helping his old friend Gert Hazen in cottage #1. Barbara and I paid only $300/month rent for many years; had free access to Dewey's fruit trees; grew our own raspberries, blackberries, pears, and apples; and tended a large organic garden on the sunny west side of our cottage. Our two cats stalked mice in the pasture, scampering to safety if Dewey's horses ambled too close. There was a brick barbeque in our back yard, a clothesline in the side yard, and a shaded front porch. For me, 1066 Terrace Drive was a paradise.

Barbara Evans (left) and Nancy Manahan (right) cleaning an area rug and chair at 1066 Terrace Drive, March 1984. *Courtesy of Nancy Manahan.*

I often went walking or birding at Tulocay Cemetery or hiked the hills behind the cemetery. From 1984–1990, Barbara and I ran Gemini, the first woman-owned carpet and upholstery-cleaning business in the Napa Valley, from our little cottage. We cleaned area rugs on the concrete slab in front of our garage and hung them to dry on the split rail fence. I remember picking up my goddaughter Caitlin from pre-school in Carneros. While I did Gemini work, she would play with the cats, climb the barbeque chimney, talk to the horses, and pick berries or ripe tomatoes. It seems that Terrace Drive was a paradise for a child, too.

Special thanks to Jay Rogers for his memories of growing up wild in rural Napa, which inspired the poem at the beginning of this essay.

Chapter 9
THE WAY WE LIVE TODAY

A FINE STATE OF PERFECTION: DR. PHONG VU'S NAPA CHILDHOOD

O white pear,
your flower-tufts,
thick on the branch,
bring summer and ripe fruits
in their purple hearts…
Hilda Doolittle, "Pear Tree"

Phong Vu tells me:

> *My family first came to Napa around 1981. There was a church in the community* [St. Appollinaris] *that had sponsored some of my other relatives to come to Napa, who had then paved the way for us to come over safely. I was around the age of one at the time. My first memory that I can recall was walking around the parking lots of the Stonehouse apartments with my mother. This was where the whole collection of us had stayed for a while until we had all gotten settled. My immediate family, which consisted of my father, mother, and older brother, then moved to a duplex on Silverado Trail located across from the Hamburger stand and what was once Vallergas. We lived in this place from about 1984 to 1989. It was during this time that I remember the pear trees from the Napa College.*

Native to temperate Europe and western Asia, pears (*Pyrus communis*) are one of the two dozen plants known to have been cultivated over four thousand years. In the fourth century BC, Homer called them the fruit of the gods. West Coast pears were originally brought by the Spanish to Mexico and traveled up the California coast with the early missions. The boom in California pear growing came after the gold rush, in the late 1800s, when farmers planted large orchards of European pears to provide fruits for a growing population. Gold seekers, when they came to Napa during the winters, were willing to pay high prices for the pleasure of eating fresh fruit.

The Thompson brothers, who traded lumber for land with Mariano Vallejo, planted fruit trees near Suscol Creek, which they diverted and channeled for irrigation. By 1860, Thompson's Gardens were known all over the West, with 150,000 fruit trees thriving. In 1869, when the transcontinental high-speed train roared to life, Napa's fruit production exploded. Napa offered the ideal climate and available land even for people who didn't have a lot of money. By 1923, the *San Francisco Chronicle* described Napa pears as reaching "a fine state of perfection." After World War II, the small, easily bruised heritage varieties were gradually eliminated in favor of a large pear that could be shipped and handled and had a long shelf life: the Bartlett. The inland coastal valleys of California, Oregon and Washington became the largest pear-growing area in the United States, producing 90 percent of the pear crop. Phong Vu recalls:

> *When we first came here to Napa from Vietnam, my father found a temporary job working on the Napa College campus. This is how I think we found out about the pear trees. For several years I remember my mother taking my brother and me to the pear orchards. At first, because I was so young, my mother would tell me to wait on the concrete while she and my brother would go pick the trees. She would tell me that there were snakes nearby, which I guess scared me enough to stay put. I've never seen a snake there in my life. Then as I got a little bit older she eventually had me help out. We'd come fully prepared with our brown paper grocery bags and just pick away, sometimes until daylight was gone. I remember the grass was always yellow and the trees looked somewhat—"scraggly"—I guess would be the best word to describe it. The pears themselves were sometimes green, sometimes yellow, and often times with worm holes in them. After we would take them home, my mom would wash them, skin them, and cut them into pieces for my brother and me. Although sweet, I remember them being somewhat of a dry texture, not like the ones you would find at the*

store these days. Often times we had picked so much that the extra pears would eventually make their way to other family households. I am surprised to hear that the trees were planted by the inmates from the Mentally Ill hospital. In fact until I was older, I had always thought the hospital was somebody's big house.

The state chose Napa in the 1870s as the site to build the 192-acre asylum because the land was so inexpensive. Approximately 204 acres of the original Tulocay Mexican land grant were purchased from Don Cayetano Juarez for $15,000. Eventually, hospital acreage totaled 2,000 from the Napa River to the eastern skyline. The early Asylum, which locals called "The Farm," was nearly self-sustaining, with live-in staff, vegetable fields, orchards, cattle, a bakery and a wharf on the Napa River to receive supplies, as well as patients who, as late as the 1920s, still made the trip up the river in wicker cages secured to the boat deck. Because the founders believed that farming would be therapeutic, patients raised all of their own vegetables, meat and dairy products and operated an award-winning pigsty. The patients also tended

The Napa Asylum opened its doors in 1876. *Courtesy of Napa County Historical Society.*

the orchards on the hospital grounds. In the late 1960s, state senator John Dunlap arranged for the transfer of these orchard lands to the newly built community college campus, next to Kennedy Park, ironically named for the first president associated with the Vietnam War. Phong Vu explains:

> *My mother and father originally left Vietnam to look for a better life for my brother and me. Like many Vietnamese people after the war, they have their own story of escape, which I don't remember, but have heard many times before through their words and the words of my other relatives who also took that journey. Through the kindness of many Good Samaritans, most of my family made it to California—some in Los Angeles, some in San Jose and some, like my own family, ended up in Napa.*

After the end of the Vietnam War, several waves of refugees from Vietnam, Cambodia and Laos were admitted to the United States; between 1983 and 1991, between 35,000 to 52,000 were admitted each year, for a

Phong Vu as a child, 1980s. *Courtesy of Phong Vu.*

total of 367,174. Andrew Lam describes what happened next: "Children are born, old folks are buried, and businesses opened. That is to say our roots sink, slowly but deeply, into the American loam." Dr. Vu recalls:

> *I have very fond memories growing up here. Fishing with homemade fishing rods in the Napa River, smashing quarters on the Wine Train tracks, circus acts at the Napa Fairgrounds, duck feeding near Kennedy park, July Fourth fireworks on the Napa College soccer field and even waking up to see people swimming in the streets during the 1986 flood. My most cherished past time, however, were the weekly gatherings at my relatives' house. Every Saturday, my mother and father would bring us to the homes of aunts and uncles where we would have Vietnamese Catholic mass. While the parents would catch up with each other's lives, the kids would play in the streets until night. It was here in these homes that our family was able to hold onto their culture. Although most of the children have grown up and moved on, the tradition is still going on till this day with new family friends. I've been truly blessed to have lived in such a wonderful community and one day look forward to having my children call this city their home.*

Dr. Vu is a practicing optometrist at the office of Drs. John Bosetti and Nancy Jameson.

MARIA'S STORY

Indigenous peoples lived in California for tens of thousands of years until it was taken by Mexico. The Californios grew citrus, fruit, corn, beans, barley, peas, mission grapes, nuts and wheat in the valleys of Sonoma and Napa. But in 1846, the United States declared a controversial war with Mexico. By 1848, Mexico had surrendered. Under the Treaty of Guadalupe Hidalgo, the United States was given possession of half of Mexico, which included much of the present southwestern United States, including California. The treaty also guaranteed Californios rights to both property and equality. Eventually, both property and equality would be lost and forgotten even though the California Constitution of 1849 was written in both Spanish and English.

During the Depression, many Mexican Americans in California were swept up and deported by train to Mexico. But when World War II began, the boom in defense jobs created a labor shortage in the agricultural industry.

Cayetano Juarez was a soldier for General Vallejo, who gave him Tulocay Rancho, where eventually Tulocay Cemetery, as well as the Asylum, would be located. *Courtesy of Napa County Historical Society.*

Lilia Navarro with three of her daughters, 1971. *Courtesy of Maria Navarro Esparza.*

In 1942, growers persuaded the federal government to create the *bracero* program in California, bringing Mexican workers to fill the labor gap. Some of them stayed and established homes in Napa. After the bracero program ended in the 1960s, other workers traveled north to pick crops that included lettuce, apples, prunes and grapes.

In 1975, farmer Nathan Fay of Rutherford hired Jose Navarro to harvest his grapes. In 1976, a panel of French judges, tasting blind, declared several California wines to be superior to their French counterparts. Chief among the winners was the '73 Stag's Leap Wine Cellars Cabernet Sauvignon. Stag's Leap was founded by Warren Winiarski, whose young vineyard was next door to Fay's and was propagated from Fay's best vines. Napa's wines would now become famous around the world.

By 1980, Mr. Fay had offered Jose Navarro a full-time job as a foreman so that he was able to bring his family—wife, Lilia, and three daughters—from Mexico. This is the story of one of those daughters, Maria Elena. She remembers:

> *I was born in the town of La Piedad, Michoacan, Mexico. When I was about four years old, my dad came to California for the first time looking for work. My mom, my sisters, Lilia and Gabriela, and I lived with my grandparents. When I was 11 years old, we moved. The separation from my grandparents proved to be too difficult for both my sisters and my grandparents, so they returned to Mexico to live with them. They would come to Napa to stay with our family in the summer and then return again to Mexico.*
>
> *When my father sent for us, we moved into an apartment on Collier Boulevard, located within walking distance from Ridgeview Junior High, which was the first school I attended when arriving here. My dad was not aware of the school enrollment procedures for getting me into school, so he went to his older brother for assistance. My uncle and his wife, Lupe Navarro, were longtime residents of Napa, where they had raised their children. Lupe took me to Napa County Health Department, and that's where I got my vaccinations prior to entering school and where I received my first immunization card.*
>
> *Because of my limited English, I was terrified of going to school. They didn't call themselves the Rebels for nothing! We Latino kids hung out together and didn't always feel welcome. Fortunately, for all of us non-English speakers, we were assigned to a first period, total immersion class with Gene Halliday, who made learning the language fun, interesting and provided a supportive learning environment. At the end of this class, we then went into regular classrooms for the rest of the school day.*
>
> *Homework assignments were difficult because of the language barrier. Susana Meza was my best friend. She helped me to get a grip on English and within six months I was doing well. I had gone to a private school*

in Mexico, which was academically ahead of schools here in Napa, so I was on the honor roll and was a straight A student. I was kept in the ESL program until I was fluent. ESL Latino kids were expected to go to summer school to increase their English proficiency. In the summer of 1985, every Saturday we went to Sonoma State University for math and English classes.

My parents became very involved in the Migrant Child Education. My sister Raquel was born in 1981. When she attended Shearer school, my mom, Lilia, created a Mexican folk dance group that eventually became known as the Napa Valley Ballet Folklorico. In 1982, Mr. Fay provided my family a house on Spencer Street to live rent-free. When he retired in 1985, in order to make sure the family had housing security, Mr. Fay deeded the house to my father.

I attended Napa High School. When it came to dating, my parents were very traditional and did not let me go out without a chaperone. My best friend was Adelina Gouveia. She was of Portuguese descent and her family shared the same values, so my friend's brothers were my chaperones when we went out. While I was in high school, Vintage High counselor Roberto

Wedding of Jorge and Maria Navarro Esparza, June 20, 1987. *Courtesy of Maria Navarro Esparza.*

> *Garcia helped me get a job working for the Molinaris. They had purchased Rossi's Deli on Main Street, a mom and pop grocery store, originally owned by Frank Rossi. I met my husband, Jorge Esparza, while in high school and got married at eighteen. Our ceremony was held at the family home on Spencer Street in 1987.*

In May 2000, Nathan Fay was honored at Stag's Leap. Describing the event for the *Los Angeles Times*, Rod Smith described how "the valley's renowned vine-budding specialist, Jose Navarro, says he learned his basic budding technique from Nathan Fay." Eugene Halliday, Maria's teacher, taught for the Napa Valley Unified School District for thirty-two years before retiring in 1990. He passed away in 2011. The Navarro family operated Jefferson Food Market from 2000 to 2006. Maria's sister Raquel Navarro graduated from UCLA, the first American-born generation of her family to complete college. Her older sisters, Lilia and Gabriela, still live in Mexico. Maria's mother, Lilia Navarro, continues to direct Napa Valley Ballet Folklorico. Maria Navarro-Esparza helped found Fair Housing of Napa Valley in 2003. Currently, she is a resident services coordinator and agricultural worker liaison at Napa Valley Community Housing. She and her husband, a member of Ironworkers Union Local 378, have recently celebrated their silver anniversary. They are the proud parents of Jorge Jr. and Nathalia. Maria remains close friends with Susana Meza.

A Collins Family Christmas

Twin sisters Sheryl and Susan have been attending their parents' Christmas Eve celebration since they can remember. Dave Collins's parents moved to Napa in 1942. They joined other family members who were already living here and bought a farm on Hedgeside Avenue in East Napa. Dave's dad worked at Mare Island. He also repaired watches from a workshop on the farm. Joan married Dave in 1957 as a young bride of eighteen. After his parents passed, in 1994 Dave and Joan moved into the Hedgeside home, where these celebrations now take place.

Christmas Eve is the special night for this family, when Joan makes her Portuguese mother's crab *cioppino* recipe. Mr. and Mrs. Collins do their best to drive every year to buy their crab fresh from Bodega Bay. Now that the children have grown, they all pitch in with purchasing and providing crab. The meal

Dave Collins with Christmas crab. *Courtesy of Susan Collins.*

includes French bread, salad and spaghetti for those who don't want crab. Every year, several dozen friends and family gather at the Collinses' home. "No matter what other commitments people have, everyone makes a point of getting to Mom and Dad's that night," says Susan. Guests may include not only family, but also boyfriends, girlfriends and even ex-husbands. Sheryl remembers Christmas Eve with her first newborn baby, Billy, in 1988. In the 1990s, their older sister, Lezlie, often brought friends who had fallen on hard times all the way from Sacramento to give them an enjoyable holiday.

As the winter evening darkens, someone lights the pink Advent candles. Sheryl pours what is now referred to as "Sheryl's Famous Eggnog," really an old Martha Stewart eggnog recipe. She offers a toast in memory of her older brother, Dave Collins II. Another special tradition is Mrs. Collins's miniature Nativity scene. Over the month of December, the Three Kings gradually make their way through the house until the baby Jesus appears in the manger by Christmas Eve dinner. After dinner, everyone gathers for "Silent Night" and "Twelve Days of Christmas." Their dad passes out song sheets and leads the singing as everyone contributes their own verses. As each of the children learned to play a musical instrument such as the trumpet, guitar and violin, they would be asked to play a song. This year, the sisters look forward to Sheryl's daughter, Hannah, playing the violin.

The evening ends when Mr. and Mrs. Collins attend Midnight Mass at St. John the Baptist Catholic Church with their grandchildren. Before church, everyone

Susan Collins on Christmas Eve. *Courtesy of Susan Collins.*

pitches in cleaning the dishes to help their mother, who has been cooking for days. Susan laughs, "It usually takes Mom a month to figure out where everything was put away."

The Collins family celebration may end at Midnight Mass, but it really begins in November when the olive trees on their property are harvested by hand. Many generations of the Collins family gather to climb ladders and pick olives from the branches. Sheryl describes how "every single olive must be inspected to make sure is doesn't have frostbite or bugs." These olives are then taken to a local winery to be pressed. Whoever attends the harvest is gifted with a special bottle of olive oil, which the family calls "liquid gold," on Christmas Eve.

This year, all of these traditions will continue. If you happen to be driving down a quiet country road known as Hedgeside Avenue, you might spot a large lighted Silver Tip pine tree outside an old farm. Sheryl and Sue have happily lived in Napa their entire lives. In a collection of Christmas music that originally sold for eighty-five cents, I found this song:

Winds through the olive trees softly did blow;
Round little Bethlehem long, long ago.
Sheep on the hillside lay whiter than snow,
Shepherds were watching them long, long ago.

May the winds blow gently through the olive trees on Hedgeside for the Collins family for many years to come.

Sheryl Collins's daughters, Hannah and Justine, picking olives. *Courtesy of Sheryl Collins.*

Sheryl's Famous Eggnog

24 eggs
2 cups granulated sugar
2 quarts whole milk
2 cups bourbon
2 cups cognac
2 quarts heavy cream
Freshly grated nutmeg.

Beat egg yolks together with sugar until mixture is creamy. Add whole milk, bourbon and cognac. Stir well. (This mixture is the eggnog base and can be made early.) Just before serving, whip cream until soft peaks form. Whip egg whites to a similar consistency separately; fold cream and egg whites into egg yolk mixture. Pour eggnog into very large bowl. Sprinkle with nutmeg. Serves 50.

Epilogue

Writing history is like sending a toy boat down a stream, never knowing what ripples it may create. After reading my article in the October 2007 *Marketplace* magazine, Judy Lloyd wrote me this letter:

> *I was born and raised in Napa, as was my mother, whose maiden name was Bergantini. The Bergantinis came to Napa from Genoa, Italy, and lived in the Italian community in Alta Heights district. In fact, I live in the house my mother grew up in, on Silverado Trail between Berna and Spring Streets. When I first moved here twenty years ago I had a great view of the Napa Garbage company—as well as a great stench carried on the evening breezes.*
>
> *What was once a quiet country road is now a traffic-packed highway. My mother used to sit on the front porch and count cars; she tells me maybe five or six would go by. When my youngest son was a toddler, we continued the tradition of counting cars—and 60 or more vehicles would pass by during our short time on the porch. My mother loves to tell stories about growing up on the Trail. Her grandmother lived just north of Spring, on the Trail, and my mother would run across the field to visit her. We never got tired of hearing about all the Italian families like the Grimoldis, Bacigalupis, Rossis, and Paniaguas, whose children grew up with her in Alta Heights.*
>
> *Your article hit home for me as my husband and I contemplate what will happen when the new proposed Ritz Carlton goes up. I feel like that*

> *little house in Virginia Lee Burton's children's book,* The Little House. *Businesses will eventually be surrounding us and the traffic will be horrendous. Of course, as a union electrician, my husband loves the growth, which creates more work.*
>
> *Regarding Pear Tree Lane, I can't help but reminisce every time I drive by the new development. I grew up just east of Beard Road, and my girlfriends and I would ride our bikes down Pear Tree Lane almost every day. It was a dirt road ending in a dead end where the orchard was. We picked pears and played in the orchard. As a young teen I would go down there to sneak a smoke...There was also a creek that ran south of Pear Tree where we would swing on willow tree branches. What lovely memories I have, memories I love to share.*
>
> *A few years ago I began to hate Napa. I was discouraged that I would never be able to afford to purchase a home in the town I was born and raised. I was tired of sharing the roads with tourists who didn't know where they were going. I despised the little expensive shops that were built solely to attract such tourists. Who cares about all that wine stuff anyway? Then a miracle happened.*
>
> *I was hired to work at Stag's Leap Winery. How did I not know this amazing property even existed. Gazing across vineyards green with the new spring, I drove through the small gate and into heaven. It was then I thought I was home. I fell in love with Stag's Leap; its people, the property, the haunted Manor House and quaint old cottages; the wine. Oh yes, now I get the whole wine thing, but most of all I fell in love with the Napa Valley.*

The winery was founded in 1893 by Horace Chase and his wife, Minnie Mizner Chase. She was the daughter of California state senator and later U.S. ambassador Lansing B. Mizner. The land was named Stag's Leap after an indigenous legend of a stag leaping across crags of the palisades (bordering the east side of the estate) to escape hunters. In addition to the old stone winery, the Chases built a manor and guesthouse that still stand. The Chase House was a masonry structure of uncoursed ashlar. A notable feature was the round turret with a castellated top. The Chase family excavated the first wine storage caves on the east side of Napa Valley and installed what is thought to be the first in-ground freshwater swimming pool in Northern California.

Stag's Leap became a place that attracted prominent politicians, artists and writers of the early twentieth century. Visitors making a journey from San Francisco crossed the Bay by ferry to Vallejo, boarded a train to

Yountville and made the last leg of their journey to Stag's Leap in horse-drawn carriages. Mrs. Frances Grange purchased the property from the Chase family in 1913; she ran the acreage as a working ranch and resort. She built some guest cottages that surrounded the main house. By the 1920s, the resort was called Stag's Leap Manor. It offered lawn tennis, swimming, horseback riding, children's activities, golf, music, cards, a library and Napa Valley wines before and after Prohibition.

Judy Lloyd's reference to Virginia Lee Burton's book reminded me of Anne Tyler's essay about *The Little House.* I cut it out twenty years ago, like so many things that I saved, never knowing that it would appear in a book someday. Tyler wrote:

> *Like a child, the Little House has its periods of restlessness. And like a child, it finds even longed-for changes both exciting and saddening. Alone at night in the city that has always seemed to beckon, "she missed the field of daisies and the apple trees dancing in the moonlight."*

Judy Lloyd finished her letter by concluding:

> *Next year, I turn 50. I still can't afford a house but that's okay for now. I will continue to live in the family home on the Trail where I will sit on the porch and count the cars. I will follow behind the tipsy tourists on my way home from work and pray for their safe trip home. I will continue to enjoy the fruits of our labor here at the winery, the history, and ghost stories. I will continue to remember Pear Tree Lane and the little grimy girls who played in the orchard.*

Notes

Chapter 1

Retracing Juliana's Path

Anderson, Fred. "America: Into the Heart of Darkness." *New York Review of Books*, April 4, 2013.

Heidenreich, Linda. *"This Land was Mexican Once": Histories of Resistance from Northern California*. Austin: University of Texas Press, 2007.

Jackson, Donald, ed. *The Journals of Zebulon M. Pike, with Letters and Related Documents.* Norman: University of Oklahoma, 1966..

Jones, Harvey, and Janice Driesbach. "Art of the Gold Rush." http://www.museumca.org/goldrush/art-intro.html.

Weber, Lin. *Old Napa Valley*. St. Helena, CA: Wine Ventures Publishing, 1998.

Yount, George. *George C. Yount and His Chronicles of the West: Comprising Extracts from the Memoirs and from the Orange Clark Narrative*. Denver, CO: Old West Publishing, 1996.

Special thanks to Tucker Catlin, who compiled much of the research on Juliana Pope based on what he learned from Joe Collizo of Pope Valley.

"The Sky's Blue Looking-Glass"

Fisher, M.F.K. "Introduction: Napa Wine." In *Silverado Squatters*. St. Helena, CA: James Beard, 1965.

Orton, Arthur. "Reconstructing the Robert Louis Stevenson Silverado Squatters Cabin." 1980.

Stevenson, Robert Louis. *A Child's Garden of Verses, 1885*. Hertfordshire, UK: Wordsworth Editions Ltd; 1994.

———. *Silverado Squatters*. St. Helena, CA: Silverado Museum, Lewis Osborne, 1974.

Transactions of the Royal Scottish Society of Arts 8 (1870–71).

Waterston, Elizabeth. "Going for Eternity: A Child's Garden of Verse." *Canadian Children's Literature* 96 (1999).

Stories of Suffrage

Anthony, Susan B. Speech at last convention on her eighty-sixth birthday. http://tcuwomensnetwork.wordpress.com/2009/11/02/failure-is-impossible-susan-b-anthony.

Kammen, Carol. *On Doing Local History*. Walnut Creek, CA: Altimira Press, 2003.

McGriff-Payne, Sharon. *John Grider's Century: African Americans in Solano, Napa and Sonoma Counties from 1845 to 1925*. Bloomington, IN: iUniverse, 2009.

Silver, Mae, and Sue Cazaly. *The Sixth Star.* San Francisco, CA: Ord Street Press, 2000.

Yerger, Rebecca. "Suffragists Met in Opera House." *Napa Register*, March 3, 1996.

CHAPTER 2

Turn-of-the-Century Downtown

Kammen, Carol. *On Doing Local History*. Walnut Creek, CA: Altimira Press, 2003.

Silver, Mae, and Sue Cazaly. *The Sixth Star.* San Francisco, CA: Ord Street Press, 2000.

A Japanese Journey

Basho, Matsuo. *Basho: The Complete Haiku*. Kodansha USA, 2008.

Napa Daily Journal, February 14, 1904.

Nishizu, Mr. Clarence Iwao. Excerpts from interview by Arthur A. Hansen for the Honorable Stephen K. Tamura Orange County Japanese American Oral History Project, June 14, 1982. Edited by Mr. Nishizu and published in 1991. Interview discovered by librarian Stephanie Grohs.

Weber, Lin. *Roots of the Present: Napa Valley, 1900 to 1950*. St. Helena, CA: Wine Ventures Publishing, 2001.

For more on Japanese contribution to California agriculture see Coodley, Lauren. *California: A Multicultural Documentary History*. Upper Saddle River, NJ: Pearson, 2008.

Time Passing in Napa

Amato, Joseph. *Rethinking Home*. Berkeley: University of California Press, 2002.

Ezettie, Louis. Articles, June/September 1961. Courtesy of the Napa County Historical Society

———. "Looking into Napa's Past and Present." *Napa Register*, August 6, 1977.

Many thanks to the Merry Mariners for sharing their observations with me on February 16, 2008.

CHAPTER 3

Voices from Early Browns Valley

Smith, Jane. Article. *Napa Register*, May 22, 1973.

Napa's Roaring Twenties

Smith, Jane. Article. *Napa Valley Register*, June 27, 1994.

A Tannery in a Town, I and II

Baskin, John. *New Burlington: The Life and Death of an American Town*. New York: W.W. Norton & Company, 2000.

Faux, Jeff. *The Global Class War: How America's Bipartisan Elite Lost Our Future—and What It Will Take to Win it Back*. New York: John Wiley & Sons, 2006.

Kammen, Carol. *On Doing Local History*. Walnut Creek, CA: Altamira Press, 2001.

Leather Supply House. "History of Leather Tanning and Its Movement into the New Millennium." http://www.leathersupplyhouse.com/new_reference_history_future.htm.

Weber, Lin. *Roots of the Present: Napa Valley, 1900 to 1950*. St. Helena, CA: Wine Ventures Publishing, 2001.

Warmest thanks to Wayne Taylor, Peter Manasse and Sharon Arnold for helping to write this history.

CHAPTER 4

Two Love Stories from Dunn Lee Manor

Amato, Joseph. *Rethinking Home*. Berkeley: University of California Press, 2002.

I would like to thank Sam Neft for hosting my visit with Mr. Nilan Kincaid and his daughter, Marilyn Robinson. Special thanks to Mr. Kincaid for sharing his beautiful memories of coming to manhood in Browns Valley.

Discovering Rita Bordwell, I and II

Bordwell, Rita. "History of the Napa Fire Department from 1859 to 1962." Available at the Napa Firefighters' Museum.

———. "Napa County Labor Movement Was Born of Depression." *Napa Register*, March 30, 1963.

Brennan, Nancy. *This Was Napa*. Napa County Historical Society, Spring 1998.

Edington, Astrid. "Firefighters Honor 'Napa's Great Lady.'" *Napa Register*, October 4, 1969.

Heilbrun, Carolyn. *Writing a Woman's Life*. New York: Norton and Company, 1988.

Napa Register. "Sixth Supervisor Rita Bordwell Dies." Obituary, February 22, 1975.

Steinbeck, John. *Their Blood is Strong*. Pamphlet, 1938.

Zinn, Howard. *Failure to Quit: Reflections of an Optimistic Historian*. Cambridge, MA: South End Press, 1993.

Every Memory a Door

Clerici, Andrew. Letter to author, 2005.

Dennis, C. Michael James. "The Circus Is in Town!" *The Critic*, 1898.

Haufellner, Schilfarth. *Elefanten in Zoo und Circus, Dokumentation 2 Nordamerika*. European Elephant Group, 1997.

Manasse, Peter. Letter to author, 2006.

Mini, Martin. *Two Families: Cavagnaro and Guisto*. Napa, CA: self-published, 1998.

Taylor, Wayne. Letter to author, 2006.

Weber, Lin. *Roots of the Present, Napa Valley, 1900–1950*. St. Helena, CA: Wine Ventures Publishing, 2001.

CHAPTER 5

Listening for Trains

Campbell, Mary. Letter to the author, February 8, 2009.
Meehan, Don. Letter to the editor. *Napa Register*, August 24, 2006.
Schmitt, Peter. "For a Sleepless Child." In *Country Airport*. Providence, RI: Copper Beech Press, 2003.
Swett, Ira, and Harry Aitken. *The Napa Valley Route*. Hollywood, CA: Interurbans, 1975.

Following the Trail

Courtney, Kevin. "Napa Pipe Plant Loads Its Final Rail Car." *Napa Register*, September 30, 2005.
Jackson, Helen Hunt. *Poems*. Charleston, SC: Nabu Press, 2010
Napa Register. Obituary: Marian Mannering. December 8, 2003.
———. Obituary: Obediah Isaiah Johnson. January 20, 2012.
———. Obituary: Rena Tennant Johnson. July 22, 2010.
———. Obituary: Wash Mannering. July 9, 1982.

The Construction of History, I and II

Amato, Joseph. *Rethinking Home*. Berkeley: University of California Press, 2002.

Thanks to Deb Jachens for sharing the box of letters and to Stephanie Grohs for assisting with their interpretation. Thanks to Marilyn Grover for sharing her memories of Beatrice Luhmann and to Lauren Ellsworth for recording Marilyn's story and helping to interpret Beatrice's handwritten memoir.

PRELUDE TO PART II

Brennan, Nancy. *This Was Napa*. Napa County Historical Society, Spring 1998.
Friedman, Larry, Rachel Friedman, Patty Langer and Cathy Mathews. Interviews by Lauren Coodley, 2003.
Soon, Herman. Obituary for Sophia Soon. *Napa Valley Register*, January 25, 2007.

CHAPTER 6

"History Isn't Always Taught Properly"

Cornell, Jerry. "In the Spotlight: Ivy Loeber's Name Synonymous with Napa Valley Historical Studies." *Napa Register*, August 5, 1959.
Doud, Jess. "The Good Old Days." *St. Helena Star*, 1967–1974.
"Ivy Loeber, Historian." *Positive Living* (Spring 1998).
Loeber, Ivy. "Report of Trip to Identify the Battlefield of Soscol Indians and White in 1836." Napa County Historical Association, 1962.
Mikolajcik, John. "American Canyon History." In *Footsteps of Time*. Vol. 1. N.d. Retrieved from www.cityofAmericanCanyon.org.
Napa County Historical Association. "A History of St. Helena: A Century of Progress." 1955.
———. "The Legend of Spanish Mustard." As told to Ivy May Loeber by her grandfather Calvin Chesterfield Griffith, Napa County pioneer, and authenticated by Edwin Markham.
Napa Register. "Valley History Her Specialty." 1968.
Sacramento Bee. "Descendant of Napa Pioneers is Historical Chairman for CFWC." January 30, 1961.

Napa's Unknown Brenda Starr

Reyna, Liz. Unpublished manuscript, n.d.
Rodriguez, Richard. "The Death of the *San Francisco Chronicle*." June 6, 2009. www.newamericamedia.org.

What West Park Was

Amato, Joseph. *Rethinking Home*. Berkeley: University of California Press, 2002.
Salazar, Carolyn. Unpublished manuscript, n.d.

CHAPTER 7

Searching for Peggy Connolly

Courtney, Kevin. "Land Trust Defends Plan for Napa Ranch." *Napa Register*, April 9, 2004.

My thanks to Carolyn Fruchtenicht, Harold Kelly, Marilyn Warnock, Lori Saxon and Roger Andrews for their assistance in restoring the Connollys to us.

Remembering Napa's Service Stations

McFee, Michael. "Service Is Our Business." In *Shinemaster*. Pittsburgh, PA: Carnegie Mellon University Press, 2006.

Stanley, Pat. Article. *Napa Register*, May 20, 2006.

For a vivid description of the first service stations in California, see the first chapter of "Oil!" in *The Land of Orange Groves and Jails—Upton Sinclair's California*, edited by Lauren Coodley. Berkeley, CA: Heyday Books, 2004.

Fancy Faire and Community Projects

Kilgallen, Tony. *Napa: An Architectural Walking Tour*. Charleston, SC: Arcadia Publishing, 2001. Kilgallen explains that in 1905, G.W. Young built a plunge bath tank, originally a wood-frame building with a tank thirty by ninety feet. In 1912, the pool was floored over by the Catholic Church, and Dominican Sisters taught classes there. In 1920, the building was remodeled, and Community Projects hung out its sign.

My deepest thanks to MaryEllen Simmons for adding this story to women's history in our town.

CHAPTER 8

Feminism Finds Napa

Barnhill, Bonnie Lee. "Around the Grapevine." UFCW Newsletter, August 1981.

Brambila, Maria. Memoir. Unpublished, 2004.

Coodley, Lauren. Article for Women's Re-Entry newsletter, 1982.

Dietiker-Yolo, Linda. Letter from Commission on the Status of Women. May 26, 1981.

Kammen, Carol. *On Doing Local History*. Walnut Creek, CA: Altamira Press, 2003.

Napa Women's Center newsletters, 1972–1975.

Sagehorn, Elizabeth. "Over Hill and Valley." *Napa Register.* October 7, 2003.

Thomas, Laura. "Michelle the Machinist." *Napa Register*, 1980.

Mrs. Brewster's Double Life

Courtney, Kevin. "Doctor's Orders: Larry Must Quit." *Napa Register*, December 9, 1998.
Friedman, Larry, and Rachel Friedman. Interview by author, 2003.
Friedman, Rachel. Interview by author, New Year's Eve 2009.
Napa Register. "Women in Business." August 29, 1986.
Weber, Lin. *Under the Vine and the Fig Tree.* St. Helena, CA: Wine Ventures Publishing, 2003.

Thanks to Lauren Ellsworth for interview assistance.

Treasures of Terrace Drive

Amato, Joseph. *Rethinking Home.* Berkeley: University of California Press, 2002.

I am grateful to Linda for her beautiful letter, which introduced me to this story. Thanks also to Jeff Green and Nancy Manahan for their contributions.

CHAPTER 9

A Fine State of Perfection

Doolittle, Hilda. *H.D. Collected Poems, 1912–1944.* New York: New Directions Publishing Corporation, 1986.
Lam, Andrew. "My Journey Home." www.pbs.org/weta/myjourneyhome/andrew/andrew_diaspora.html.
Vu, Dr. Phong. E-mail to author, October 2009

Maria's Story

Greenberg, Amy. *A Wicked War: Poll, Clay, Lincoln, and the 1846 U.S. Invasion of Mexico.* New York: Knopf, 2012.
Heidenreich, Linda. *This Land Was Mexican Once: Histories of Resistance from Northern California.* Austin: University of Texas, 2007.
Smith, Rod. "The Man Who Made Stags Leap." http://articles.latimes.com/2000/may/10/food/fo-28362.

A Collins Family Christmas

Schaum, John W. "Winds Through the Olive Trees." *Christmas Album.* Belwin, Inc., n.d.

My thanks to Susan Hamilton and to Sheryl Collins for sharing their memories and photographs.

EPILOGUE

Lloyd, Judy, to Lauren Coodley. Correspondence, October 2007.

"Pacific Coast Architecture Database. "Chase, Horace Blanchard and Minnie Mizner Chase, House." https://digital.lib.washington.edu/architect/structures/10001.

Stag's Leap. "History: Legends of Bootleggers and Gangsters, Ghosts and Gypsies." http://stagsleap.com/estate/history.

Tyler, Anne. "Why I Still Treasure the Little House." *New York Times*, November 9, 1986.

About the Author

Lauren Coodley was born in Los Angeles, where her maternal grandparents settled in 1920. She attended high school in Bakersfield and graduated from the University of California–Berkeley. She has two master's degrees, in psychology and history, from Sonoma State University, earned twenty years apart.

She taught at Napa's community college for her entire adult life, usually classes she created, including math anxiety, women's history, children's literature and California history. She was twice elected president of the faculty, received the Distinguished Teaching Award for 2003 and was elected chair of social sciences in 2004, 2007 and 2009. Since her retirement in 2010, she is caring for her grandsons and continuing her writing career.

Her published works include: *Napa: The Transformation of an American Town* (Arcadia, 2004, revised 2007); *Land of Orange Groves and Jails: Upton Sinclair's California* (Heyday, 2004); *California: A Multicultural Documentary History* (Pearson, 2008); *Napa Valley Farming* (co-author Paula Amen Judah, Arcadia, 2011); and *Upton Sinclair: California Socialist, Celebrity Intellectual* (University of Nebraska, 2013).